AF531735

# ACHIEVEMENT MOTIVATION AND ACADEMIC ACHIEVEMENT OF ALCOHOLIC AND NON-ALCOHOLIC COLLEGE STUDENTS

# ACHIEVEMENT MOTIVATION AND ACADEMIC ACHIEVEMENT OF ALCOHOLIC AND NON-ALCOHOLIC COLLEGE STUDENTS

*By*

**Mr. K. Srinivasulu**

*M.A. (Litt.), M.Ed., P.G.C.T.E., M.Phil. (Edn)*

*Assistant Prohibition and Excise Superintendent*

*Guntur 522002*

*Andhra Pradesh*

*Editor*

**Dr. Digumarti Bhaskara Rao**

*M.Sc., M.A., M.A., M.Ed., Ph.D.*

*Principal & Research Director*

*R.V.R. College of Education*

*D-43 (277) S.V.N. Colony*

*Guntur - 522 006*

*&*

*Member, Board of Studies in Education*

*Acharya Nagarjuna University*

*digumartibhaskararao@rediffmail.com*

**DISCOVERY PUBLISHING HOUSE PVT. LTD.**

**NEW DELHI-110 002**

*Published by:*
**Tilak Wasan**
**DISCOVERY PUBLISHING HOUSE PVT. LTD.**
4383/4A, Ansari Road, Darya Ganj
New Delhi-110 002 (India)
*Phone* : +91-11-23279245, 43596064-65
*Fax* : +91-11-23253475
*E-mail* : parul.wasan@gmail.com
discoverypublishinghouse@gmail.com
*web* : www.discoverypublishinggroup.com

***First Edition:* 2012**

**ISBN: 978-93-5056-063-1**

**ACHIEVEMENT MOTIVATION AND ACADEMIC ACHIEVEMENT OF ALCOHOLIC AND NON-ALCOHOLIC COLLEGE STUDENTS**



***Printed at:***
***Shree Balaji Art Press***
***Delhi***

## *Dedicated to Esteemed Administrators*

**Mr. M. VEERA BRAHMAM,** *I.A.S.*
*Collector & District Magistrate*
*Vizianagaram*
*(Andhra Pradesh)*

**Mrs. M. VIJAYA LAKSHMI,** *M.Phil.*
*Special Grade Deputy Collector*
*Visakhapatnam*
*(Andhra Pradesh)*

# Preface

Achievement motivation is the desire of a person to meet certain standards of excellence. Academic achievement is one's learning attainments, accomplishments or proficiencies in performing a given task in education.

Alcoholism is usually referred to as excessive drinking or dependence on alcoholic beverages. Several people drink for many reasons and in many ways, situations and styles, but they should not be considered as alcoholics. Alcoholics are excessive drinkers whose dependence on alcohol has attained such a degree that they show noticeable mental disturbance or an interference with their mental and bodily health, their interpersonal relations, and their smooth social and economic functioning.

The college students, mostly, professional course students, need to keep themselves away from alcohol so as to be good students and settle well in their lives and professions when they roll out of the colleges. Unfortunately, now-a-days, many a student around the globe has become prey to alcohol due to several reasons. Hence, this study is carried out on the achievement motivation and academic achievement of alcoholic and non-alcoholic college students.

The alcoholism has shown its effect on the achievement motivation and academic achievement. The alcoholics are with lesser achievement motivation and academic achievement when compared to the achievement motivation and academic achievement of non-alcoholics.

The college, family and community should take care of the students who study in educational institutions in order to keep them away form alcoholics. The students should also stay away from alcohol and alcoholic friends. The students should have high achievement motivation to get high academic achievement.

**Dr. Digumarti Bhaskara Rao**
digumartibhaskararao@rediffmail.com
Tele-Mobile: +91 949 3333 555

# Contents

# Introduction

"Underage drinking and excessive drinking have negative effects on everything".

*—Dr. Judith Ramaley*

## INTRODUCTION

The behaviour of any individual lies in motivation. He behaves as he does because he is motivated to do so. Motivation, thus, be regarded as something which prompts, compels and energizes an individual to act or behave in a particular manner at a particular time for attaining some specific goal or purpose. The motivation in academic line promotes achievement motivation, which is responsible for good academic achievement. An academic achievement is something you do or achieve at school, college or university — in class, laboratory, library or fieldwork. It does not include sport or music.

An academic achievement, such as graduating First in one's class, is sometimes a purely quantitative matter, while having the findings of lengthy, comprehensive research published by a recognized journal is also a notable academic achievement. Being named head/chairman of a particular department at a university is both a professional and an academic achievement.

## Achievement Motivation

It has been noticed that all living organisms, whether animals or human beings are always active. In order to appreciate this fact, we only need to turn our heads around. We find that everybody is engaged in doing one thing or other. We notice that they are not doing these things in a haphazard manner, rather, their activities are directed towards attaining certain goals. People choose goals and pursue them vigorously. They plan and undertake a variety of activities. A close observation of behaviours of fellow beings would reveal that not only two different people behave differently in the same situation but also the same person behaves or performs at different levels in different occasions. It appears that variety of differences in human behaviour is a rule. Psychologists and lay people are equally interested in knowing the causes of these variations in behaviour. They are eager to know why some students do well in school while others, equally intelligent, fail. Why do some people work harder than others? Why do we do what we do? What determines our behaviour? Psychologists, here, have used the term 'motivation'.

Motivation is a generic term referring to a family of concepts used to explain initiating, direction, maintenance, and termination of activities undertaken by living organisms. It impels or pushes the organism into activity, giving them direction. It is useful to explain the variability observed in behaviour. In particular, the choice of behaviour is the main question because living beings are always active. The fluctuation or change in preference for activity or choice of goal leads to choosing one activity over the other. In general, people approach certain goals or engage in activities that are expected to have desirable outcomes and avoid activities that lead to unpleasant or aversive outcomes. However, many people, do like challenges, undertake difficult tasks and seek pleasure in engaging in adventures. These persons have different kinds and levels of motivation.

Achievement motivation refers to the desire of a person to meet certain standards of excellence. The need to achieve, also known as n-Arch, energises and directs behaviour and influences perception of situations. It is not biological but shows a tremendous effect on human behaviour. People differ in the degree to which they experience this need. Early studies conducted by McClelland (1961) and other researchers around the globe on achievement motivation are correlated with high scholastic performance and success in business. Such motivated people opt for moderately difficult tasks. They are future-oriented and persist more on the task. Also, they are upwardly mobile. McClelland found that, in general, protestant countries, where independence and achievement are valued, were economically more advanced. The parents train children to be self supportive and develop greater autonomy. Some researchers have found that females experience a fear of success, since striving for success may reduce feminity in the eyes of others.

Achievement motivation is acquired by children during the formative stages of social development. They learn it from their parents, other role models and socio-cultural influences. They acquire the values that they should attain a good position, social standing and distinguished status in the society.

The basis of achievement motivation is achievement motive, i.e., a motive to achieve. Those who engage themselves in a task on account of an achievement motive are said to work under the spirit of achievement motivation. Therefore, in order to understand the meaning of the term achievement motive, it is essential to know in detail the nature and meaning of achievement motive. Motives, can be classified into various types, when one is concerned with making and retaining friendship with opposite sex, we say he has sex motive, when a student desires to become monitor of his class or captain of the foot ball team, he is said to possess power motive and his desire to seek the reward and approval of his teachers or parents is termed as approval motive. Similarly, the desire to improve his performance at school or to get a good grade or to become an engineer and so on is known as achievement motive.

## Academic Achievement

The term academic achievement can be understood as one's learning attainments, accomplishments or proficiencies in performing a given task in education. Achievement is directly related to the growth and development of students in educational situations, where teaching and learning go hand-in-hand. The concept of achievement involves the interaction of three factors, viz., aptitude for learning, readiness for learning and opportunity for learning. The concept also involves health and physical fitness, motives and desires and emotional balances of the individuals in the fulfillment of the given tasks. Achievement in education implies one's knowledge, understanding or skills in a specified subject or a group of subjects.

Education plays a vital role in building the society. A modern society cannot achieve its aim of economic growth, technical development and cultural advancement without fully harnessing the talents of its citizens. Educationists, thus, strive to fully develop the intellectual potential of the students and make efforts to see that their potentialities are fully realized and channelised for the benefit of the individuals and that of the society.

Educational opportunities, though open to all, do not seem to engage to any reasonable extent the capabilities of those who seek to avail of them. An eternal question baffling parents, educators and national planners is why do students of demonstrated ability flop in their academic efforts at school or college examinations? Academic under-achievement, more than academic failure, constitutes a grave problem as it amounts to wastage of human resources that is considered as an irreparable loss to society, which a developing country can ill afford. This stimulated a number of researchers to undertake studies on factors influencing academic achievement.

The situations and the environments in which the learning is to be made by the learner influence the learning process. A well equipped healthy class-room environment proves a motivating force. The child likes to read, write or listen to the teacher carefully if he finds favourable environment and appropriate learning situations. The suitability of the building, the seating arrangement and other physical facilities available and affection he gets from his teachers, the mutual cooperation and help he gets from his class-mates, the opportunity or participation he gets in the co-curricular activities, etc., will influence and motivate the learning behaviour of the child. Therefore, efforts should be made to provide suitable learning situations and environment for effective learning and enhancement of academic achievement and achievement motivation.

Super (1949) pointed out that there exists a relationship between intelligence and educational achievement. Emmett (1945) concluded that intelligence is the best predictor of academic success. Jordon (1923), Thurstone (1925), Toops (1926), McPhail (1927), Chauncey (1929), Edds and McCall (1933), Hartson and Sprow (1941), Durffinger (1943), Egsenck (19647) and Harper (1967) have reported significant correlation between intelligence and scholastic success.

## Alcoholism

Alcohol, a popular name for ethanol or ethyl alcohol, has been and continues to be the most widely used drug. People have been drinking alcohol for perhaps since 15,000 years. In ancient India, the consumption of alcohol, though permitted for religious and medical purposes, was forbidden for those belonging to higher castes and women. During the Moghul period, under Babar's reign, consumption of alcohol was widely prevalent. However, fearing defeat in battles, Babar prohibited the drinking of alcohol in his army and court. He himself kept strictly away from alcohol.

Before independence, in 1937, the Indian National Congress adopted prohibition as part of its programme, to protect the weaker sections against the economically deteriorating effects of alcohol. Prohibition was also introduced as a directive principle in the constitution. The states of Madras, Bombay and Sourastra also introduced prohibition. In the Madras State (now Tamil Nadu), except for a brief period of three years between 1971 and 1974, there has been continuous prohibition. In Andhra Pradesh also, there was prohibition for some time, but now alcohol is consumed at will and pleasure as it is available abundantly.

From this brief outline, it may be noted that drinking has been prevalent in India from ancient times and prohibition of alcohol has been introduced at different times for different reasons — religious, moral, military, social, economic and political; whatever may be the reasons for prohibition, the underlying factor that alcohol affects individuals, families and societies has been well recognized.

Alcoholism is usually referred to as excessive drinking or dependence on alcoholic beverages which people drink for many reasons and in many ways, situations and styles. They should not be considered as alcoholics. The World Health Organisation (WHO) has defined alcoholics as "excessive drinkers whose dependence on alcohol has attained such a degree that they show noticeable mental disturbance or an interference with their mental and bodily health, their interpersonal relations, and their smooth social and economic functioning or who show the prodromal (beginning) signs of such developments".

Alcohol is a central nervous system depressant. It decreases inhibitions and thus increases some behaviours that are normally under tight control. Alcohol is absorbed into the blood stream from stomach and small intestine. It is absorbed rapidly if the stomach is empty. Mixing alcohol with water slows the absorption process, but adding soda or water to alcohol speeds it up.

The effects of alcohol vary with the amount of alcohol in the blood stream and with the weight and gender of the user. The behaviour of the individuals who have consumed alcohol is highly correlated to blood alcohol levels. With increasing amounts of alcohol in the blood stream, people typically exhibit progressively slowed behaviour, often they show severe motor disturbances such as staggering.

People drink alcoholic beverages for a variety of reasons. As a depressant, alcohol helps people get rid themselves from tension and anxiety. In doing so, they move from a state of active consciousness to once in which their tension is relieved.

Alcoholism is a chronic, progressive and often fatal disease. It is a primary disorder and not a symptom of other diseases or emotional problems. The alcohol consumption can be categorized into moderate drinking, hazardous (heavy) drinking and harmful drinking. The chemistry of alcohol allows it to affect nearly every type of cell in the body, including those in the central nervous system. After prolonged exposure to alcohol, the brain adapts to the changes that alcohol makes and becomes dependent on it. The severity of the disease is influenced by factors such as genetics, psychology, culture and response to physical pain.

Genetic factors play a significant role in alcoholism and may account for about half of the total risk for alcoholism. Genes that regulate certain chemical byproducts of alcohol are under intense scrutiny. Alcohol is metabolized in a two-stage process: it is first converted to acetaldehyde (AcH), which is then converted into acetate. Acetate is toxic and in high amounts of it cause to flushing, dizziness, and nausea. Individuals with this genetic factor, then, are less likely to become alcoholic.

Alcohol releases the neurotransmitters (chemical messengers in the brain) like the Dopamine, Serotonine and Opioid peptides and other chemicals that produce pleasurable feelings. The media portrays the pleasure of drinking in advertising and programming. The medical benefits of light to moderate drinking are frequently publicized, giving ex-drinkers the spurious excuse of returning to alcohol for their health.

Signs of alcoholism or alcohol dependence include the following:

- The only indication of early alcoholism may be the unpleasant physical responses to withdrawal that occur during even brief periods of abstinence.
- Alcoholics have little or no control over the quantity they drink or the duration or frequency of their drinking.
- They are preoccupied with drinking, deny their own addiction and continue to drink even though they are aware of the dangers.
- Overtime, some people become tolerant to the effects of drinking and require more alcohol to become intoxicated, creating the illusion that they can hold their liquor.
- They have blockouts after drinking and frequent hangovers that cause them to miss work and other normal activities.
- Alcoholics might drink alone and start early in the day.
- They periodically quit drinking or switch from hard liquor to beer or wine, but these periods rarely last.
- Severe alcoholics often have a history of accidents, marital and work instability and alcohol related health problems.
- Episodic violent and abusive incidents involving spouses and children and a history of unexplained or frequent accidents are often signs of drug or alcohol abuse.

Alcoholism can develop incidentally and often there is no clear link between problem drinking and alcoholism. Eventually, alcohol dominates thinking, emotions and actions and becomes the primary means through which a person can deal with people, work and life. Alcohol can affect the body in so many ways that researchers are having a hard time determining exactly what the consequences are from drinking. It is well known, however, that chronic consumption leads to many problems, some of them deadly. It is a particular danger for adolescents who may want to impress their friends with their ability to drink alcohol but cannot yet gauge its effects. Adult children of alcoholic parents are at higher risk for divorce and for psychiatric symptoms.

Drinking too much alcohol can cause mild neurological problems including insomnia and headache. Long-term alcohol use may physically affect the brain. Brain scans of people with long-term alcoholism have shown atrophy in different parts of the brain and reduced brain activity. People with alcoholism tend to have lifestyles that put them at higher risk for hepatitis B and C and problems in the gastrointestinal tract. The effects of alcohol on heart disease and stroke vary depending on consumption. Cardiovascular disease is the leading cause of death in alcoholics. Cancer is the second leading cause of death in alcoholics. Alcoholism reduces levels of the male hormone testosterone, contributing to impotency in men.

## Academic Achievement and Achievement Motivation

Academic achievement and achievement motivation are inter-related and need a careful attention from teachers and students.

- Goals and purposes should be clearly mentioned to students.
- Material reinforces and verbal reinforces are to be judiciously used, whether positive or negative.

- False incentives should be avoided.
- Learning experiences should have some relevance and value.
- Students' learning is to be encouraged.
- Success leads to realistic goals. The more positive the teachers approach is and more pleasurable the associations are the higher would be the level of motivation.
- To promote greater educational attention to individual needs of students and to make best use of attractive abilities, their interests and expertise in teacher's community.
- To make the class-room teaching effective according to the interests and capacities of the pupil.
- To encourage flexibility in grouping the students. In this, the grouping of the students in a subject is done according to the interests and aptitudes of the students.
- To increase the quality of the instruction.
- To develop community sense.
- To conserve and promote the Indian culture and civilization.
- To involve the individuals in the social welfare.
- To evaluate whether the students are really deriving greater educational value from the 'enriched' and 'vitalized' programme than they do formally.
- To re-establish faculty 'esprit de corps' and school morale to assess in various ways the degree of improvement in personal and professional attitudes in human relations.
- To estimate the success with which guidance procedures, differentiated programmes of study, courses and units of learning experience,

individualized teaching and learning procedures and other educational measures designed to achieve greater satisfaction of individual needs.

- To realize the fact that the so called general intelligence tests are not actually general but it measures some specific abilities.
- To achieve desirable goals by meaningfully involving teachers in making and carrying out plans that effect intelligence and personality, providing an atmosphere of acceptance, support and understanding, and helping people experience feelings of warmth, helping people make sound judgement and act on the basis of careful study of adequate and accurate information.
- Do everything possible to improve student's physical condition. Various studies have shown that improvements in health may lead to marked gains in IQ scores as well as in capacity for steady intellectual growth.
- Make certain that students have maximum opportunity for achieving new and higher quality perception. Perception occurs only when a meaning is grasped.
- The capacity of a person to improve his perceptions may be increased of some of his most pressing goals are met.
- We can help the student to achieve more useful perceptions independently, which helps in fostering academic achievement and achievement motivation.
- Schools should do what they can to help children achieve adequate concepts of self.
- Teachers and counselors should make every possible attempt to relieve threat whenever it is suspected that a child is handicapped in his perceptions.

Considering the importance and the very role of achievement motivation and academic achievement of student's life, this study has been undertaken to assess the levels of achievement motivation and academic achievement of alcoholic and non-alcoholic college students.

## STATEMENT OF THE PROBLEM

*"A Study of Achievement Motivation and Academic Achievement of Alcoholic and Non-Alcoholic College Students"*.

## NEED OF THE STUDY

Now-a-days, taking liquor has become a fashion. Some students at highest levels are also habituated to consume liquor and due to this, the academic achievement of college students is gradually decreasing. Therefore, alcoholism has become detrimental to score high marks and their academics. The habit of consumption of alcohol influences negatively to some extent on the academic achievement and achievement motivation of alcoholic and non-alcoholic college students.

The tradition of drinking has developed into a kind of culture, belief and custom, entrenched in every level of college students' environment, particularly in the West and advanced metropolis. Customs handed down through generations of college drinkers reinforce students' expectation that alcohol is a necessary ingredient for social success. These beliefs and the expectations they engender exert a powerful influence over students' behaviour towards alcohol.

Customs that promote college drinking also are embedded in numerous levels of students' environments. The walls of college sports arenas carry advertisements from alcohol industry sponsors. Alumni carry on the alcohol tradition, perhaps less flamboyantly than during their college years, at sports events and alumni social functions. Communities permit establishments near campus to serve or sell alcohol, and these establishments depend on the college clientele for their financial success.

Students deprive their expectations of alcohol from their environment and from each other, as they face the insecurity of establishing themselves in a new social milieu. Environmental and peer influences combine to create a culture of drinking. This culture actively promotes drinking, or passively promotes it, through tolerance, or even tacit approval, of college drinking as a right of passage.

A student with a high achievement orientation shows high motivation and learning. Praise is a more powerful motivator than either blame or reproof of the work performance of students. Interpretations of success and failure by students in terms of their level of aspiration, also influences motivation. The learning style of a student is likewise related to his motivational disposition.

So, teacher educators, administrators, policy planners and guidance personnel connected with educational programmes should think ways and means of reducing the alcoholism in college students and inculcating motivation in them for their better academic achievement so that they can step out of the college as responsible citizens of the nation and their importance and key role to the future generations.

## SCOPE OF THE STUDY

The present study is confined to Guntur district, Andhra Pradesh. The sample selected for the study was alcoholic and non-alcoholic college students who were studying in colleges of arts, medical, engineering, computers and management. The sample size chosen for the study was 500 (five hundred) college students studying in different colleges.

The variables chosen for the study were the alcoholic and non-alcoholic college students of arts (M.A.), medical (M.B.B.S.), engineering (B.Tech.), computers (M.C.A.) and management (M.B.A.).

The other factors that contribute to the present study, viz., socio-economic status, home background, age, creativity, personality, birth order, intelligence, adjustment, attitudes (students as well as parents), other branches of study like the M.Sc., M.Com., undergraduation, etc., were not taken into consideration because of lack of time. So, the researcher has confined the study to the alcoholic and non-alcoholic college students of arts (MA), medical (MBBS), engineering (BTech), computers (MCA), and management (MBA).

## OBJECTIVES OF THE STUDY

The objectives proposed for the study were:

1. To find out the academic achievement of college students.
2. To find out the academic achievement of alcoholic and non-alcoholic arts students.
3. To find out the academic achievement of alcoholic and non-alcoholic medical students.
4. To find out the academic achievement of alcoholic and non-alcoholic engineering students.
5. To find out the academic achievement of alcoholic and non-alcoholic computer students.
6. To find out the academic achievement of alcoholic and non-alcoholic management students.
7. To find out the achievement motivation of college students.
8. To find out the achievement motivation of alcoholic and non-alcoholic arts students.
9. To find out the achievement motivation of alcoholic and non-alcoholic medical students.
10. To find out the achievement motivation of alcoholic and non-alcoholic engineering students.
11. To find out the achievement motivation of alcoholic and non-alcoholic computer students.
12. To find out the achievement motivation of alcoholic and non-alcoholic management students.

13. To find out the difference in the academic achievement of alcoholic and non-alcoholic college students.
14. To find out the difference in the achievement motivation of alcoholic and non-alcoholic college students.
15. To find out the correlation between academic achievement and achievement motivation of alcoholic and non-alcoholic college students.
16. To find out the correlation between academic achievement and achievement motivation of alcoholic and non-alcoholic arts students.
17. To find out the correlation between academic achievement and achievement motivation of alcoholic and non-alcoholic medical students.
18. To find out the correlation between academic achievement and achievement motivation of alcoholic and non-alcoholic engineering students.
19. To find out the correlation between academic achievement and achievement motivation of alcoholic and non-alcoholic computer students.
20. To find out the correlation between academic achievement and achievement motivation of alcoholic and non-alcoholic management students.

## Educational Implications

Learning students should begin with actual life situations for proper motivation. They should have intrinsic motivation to express themselves, to explore the environment and to satisfy their curiosity.

Goals and purposes should be clearly mentioned to students. Material reinforcers and verbal reinforcers are to be judiciously used, whether positive or negative. False incentives should be avoided. Learning experiences are more meaningful when they are related to the individual's interests, when they are involved in his living, when they not only contribute to his purposes at the time but enable him to make more intelligent adjustments in the future, when they involve discovery and problem solving rather than formal drill or — mere memorization and when they result in satisfying social relations. If learning experiences have some relevance and value, students learning is encouraged. Success leads to realistic goals. The more positive the teacher's approach is and the more pleasurable the associations are, the higher would be their level of motivation.

**The Present Study**

1. Provides research-based information about the nature and extent of dangerous drinking to college administrators and students, parents, community leaders, policy makers, researchers and members of the retail beverage industry.
2. Offers recommendations to university vice-chancellors and registrars and college presidents and secretaries on the potential effectiveness of current strategies to reverse the culture of drinking.
3. Offers suggestions to the research community, including NIAAA (National Institute on Alcohol Abuse and Alcoholism), for further research on preventing hazardous college student drinking.
4. Promotes integrating research into college alcohol programme, planning requires the active participation of college and university authorities, cooperation from the larger campus community including faculty, staff and the surrounding community.
5. Helps in research on college alcoholism and in establishing effective preventive programme.

2

# Review of Related Literature

"Decisions about alcohol consumption are not just individual, they can affect the common life of the university".

—*Edward A. Malloy*

Any worthwhile research study in any field of knowledge requires an adequate familiarity with the work which has already been done in the same area. A summary of the writings of recognized authorities and of previous research provides evidence that the researcher is familiar with what is already known and what is still unknown and untested. Since effective research is based upon past knowledge, this step helps to eliminate the duplication of what has been done, and provides useful hypotheses and helpful suggestions for significant investigation.

Citing studies that show substantial agreement and those that seem to present conflicting conclusions helps to sharpen and define understanding of existing knowledge in the problem area, provides a background for the research project and makes the researcher aware of the status of the issue. Parading a long list of annotated studies relating to the problem is ineffective and inappropriate. Only those studies that are plainly relevant, competently executed and accurately reported should be included. (Bhaskara Rao)

Capitalizing on the review of expert researchers can be fruitful in providing helpful ideas and suggestions. While review articles that summarize related studies are useful, they do not provide a satisfactory substitute for an independent research. Even though the review of related literature is not a substitute for an independent work, it is one of the first steps in the research process. It is a valuable guide to define the problem, to recognize its significance, to suggest promising data gathering devices, to appropriate the study design, and sources of data for effective analysis and to arrive at fruitful conclusions. (B.V. Kumari and D. Bhaskara Rao, 2000).

The search for related literature is a time consuming process, even though it is necessary, as earlier stated, for a good research work. Hence, this chapter on Review of Related Literature is meant for the study of literature rated to academic achievement and achievement motivation.

Achievement is one's learning attainments, accomplishments or proficiencies in performing a given task. Achievement is directly related to the growth and development of students in educational situations, where teaching and learning go hand-in-hand. The achievement involves the interaction of three factors, viz., aptitude for learning, readiness for learning, and opportunity for learning. The achievement also involves health and physical fitness, motives and desires, and emotional balances of the individuals in the fulfillment of given tasks. Achievement in education implies one's knowledge, understanding or skills in a specified subject or a group of subjects.

Achievement motivation refers to the desire of a person to meet standards of excellence. The need to achieve, also known as n-Arch, energizes and directs behaviour and influences perception of situations. It is not biological but has a tremendous effect on human behaviour. People differ in the degree to which they experience this need.

## THEORETICAL PERSPECTIVES

The awareness about academic achievement and achievement motivation makes the researcher do well in his study.

### Motivation

The word motivation has been derived from the Latin word 'motum', which means to move, motor and motion. Motivation is an internal force which accelerates a response or behaviour. Some learners learn the same subject matter or task more effectively than others, some find it more rewarding and interesting than others; and some enjoy it more than others. At any given time, learners vary in the extent to which they are willing to direct their energies to the attainment of goals, due to difference in motivation.

Motivation is a generic term referring to a family of concepts used to explain initiating, direction, maintenance and termination of activities undertaken by living organisms. It impels or pushes organism into activity, giving it direction. It is useful to explain the variability observed in behaviour. In particular, the choice of behaviour is the main question because living beings are always active. The fluctuation or change in preference for activity or choice of goal leads to choosing one activity over the other. In general, people approach certain goals or engage in activities that are expected to have desirable outcomes and avoid activities that lead to unpleasant or aversive outcomes. However, many people do like challenges, undertake difficult tasks and seek pleasure in engaging in adventures. These persons have different kinds and levels of motivation.

Arun Monappa and Mirza S. Saiyadin defined motivation as the level of desire of an individual to behave in a certain matter at a certain time and in a certain situation.

Bernard said that motivation is the stimulation of actions towards a particular objective where previously there was little or no attraction to that goal.

Blair, Jones and Simpson stated that motivation is a process in which the learner's internal energies or needs are directed towards various goals and objects in his environment.

Carroll (1969) said that a need gives rise to one or more motives. A motive is a rather specific process which has been learned. It is directed towards a goal.

Crow and Crow (1962) opined that motivation is considered with the arousal of the interest in learning and to that extent is basic to learning.

Good defined motivation as the process of arousing, sustaining and regulating activity.

Guilford (1950) stated that motivation is a motive in any particular internal factor or condition that tends to initiate and sustain activity.

Harold Koontz and Cyril O'Donnell defined motivation as the drive and effort to satisfy a want or goal.

Hebb (1975) felt that motivation refers to existence of an organized phase sequence, to its direction and content, and to its persistence in given direction or stability of content.

Kelly (1955) explained that motivation is the central factor in the effective management of the process of learning. Some type of motivation must be present in all learning.

Lovell defined motivation more formally as psycho-psychological or internal process initiated by some need which leads to activity which will satisfy that need.

Maslow (1954) stated that motivation is constant, never ending, fluctuating and complex and that it is an almost universal characteristic of, particularly, every organismic state of affairs.

Rasen, Fox and Gregory (1972) defined motivation as a readiness or disposition to respond in some ways and not others to a variety of situations.

Skinner (1947) stated that motivation in school learning involves arousing, persisting, sustaining and directing desirable behaviour.

Thus, motivation is an indispensable technique for learning. It energizes and accelerates the behaviour of learner. Desirable changes in learner's behaviour are only possible when a learner is properly motivated. No learning is possible without motivation.

Success and achievement in life and learning depends very largely on how much one really wants to succeed and achieve, what cost of human effort and energy one is willing to bear to reach his goal and what strong satisfaction he looks forward to when he accomplishes his desire. In other words, an individual's success and achievement in life and learning depends on his motivation. Motivation arouses interest in learning. It is the central factor in effective management of the process of learning. If a child is motivated properly, he will have adequate achievement motivation. Achievement motivation may be associated with a variety of goals. In general, the behaviour adopted will involve an activity which is directed towards the attainment of some standard of excellence.

The characteristics of motivation are:

1. Motivation is a psycho-physiological phenomenon.
2. Motivation initiates or sustains learner's activity.
3. Motivation orients and directs the responses of the learner towards the desired objectives.
4. Motivation controls and regulates the learner's response.
5. Motivation provides the energy and accelerates the behaviour of the learner.

6. Motivation releases the tension and satisfies the needs of the learner.
7. Motivation is the internal condition or process or factor of the learner.

The functions of motivation are:

1. Motivation energies the behaviour of the learners.
2. Motivation initiates and sustains the activities of the learners.
3. Motivation initiates and sustains the behaviour of the learners.
4. Motivation accelerates the rate of activity of the learner.
5. Motivation accelerates the rate of behaviour of the learner.
6. Motivation controls the activities of the learner.
7. Motivation controls the behaviour of the learner.

## Achievement Motivation

Achievement motivation is relatively a new concept in the world of motivation. It is essentially a type of motivation that is personal in nature. It owes its birth to U.S.A. and basically a product of a system that is based on capitalism, cut throat competition, and blind race toward materialism

The basis of achievement motivation is achievement motive, i.e., a motive to achieve. Those who engage themselves in a task on account of an achievement motive are said to work under the spirit of achievement motivation. Therefore, in order to understand the meaning of the term achievement motive, it is essential to know in detail the nature and meaning of achievement motive.

Motives can be classified into various types. When one is concerned with making and retaining friendship with opposite sex, we say he has sex motive. When a student desires to become monitor of his class or captain of the football team, he is said to possess power motive and his desire to seek the reward and approval of his teachers or parents is termed as approval motive. Similarly the desire to improve his performance at school or to get a good grade or to become an engineer and so on is known as achievement motive.

Achievement was initially recognized as an important source of human motivation by the American psychologist Henry Murray in late 1930s. Although Murray identified achievement motivation as important to the behaviour of many people, it was the American psychologists David McClelland and John Atkinson who devised a way of measuring differences in achievement motivation.

McClelland, et. al. (1953) defined achievement motivation as a competition with a standard of excellence.

Achievement motivation refers to the desire of a person to meet standards of excellence. The need to achieve, also known as n-Arch, energizes and directs the behaviour and influences the perception of situations. It is not biological but shows a tremendous effect on human behaviour. People differ in the degree to which they experience this need.

Achievement motivation is acquired by children during the formative stages of social development. They learn it from their parents, other role models and socio-cultural influences. They acquire the values that they should attain a good position, social standing and distinguished status in the society.

The achievement motive is conceived as a latent disposition which is manifested in overt striving only when the individual perceives performance as instrumental to a sense of personal accomplishment (Atkinson and Feather, 1966). Achievement motive is defined in terms of the way an individual orients himself towards objects or conditions that he does not possess. If he values those objects and conditions and he feels that he ought to possess them, he may be regarded as having an achievement motive (Irving Sarnoff). A system of good direction in human activity that is closely related to competence, aggressiveness and dominance is described by psychologists as achievement motivation (McDavid and Hasari). Achievement motivation may be associated with three varieties of goals, but, in general, the behaviour adopted will involve an activity which is directed towards the attainment of some standard of excellence. Competition with other- in which they are beaten, may be included in it (McClelland and Atkinson). In general, achievement motivation is an expectancy of finding satisfaction in mastery of difficult and challenging performances whereas in the field of education, in particular, it stands for the pursuit of excellence.

Achievement motive comes into picture when an individual knows that his performance will be evaluated, that the consequence of his actions will be either a success or a failure and that good performance will produce a feeling of pride in accomplishment. Hence, achievement motive may be considered as a disposition to approach success or a capacity for taking pride in accomplishment when success at one or another activity is achieved.

Contrary to the achievement motive, there is also an aversion tendency known as 'avoidance motive' — found in the human beings. The avoidance motive or the motive to avoid failure is considered a disposition to avoid failure and/ or a capacity for experiencing shame and humiliation as a consequence of failure. Therefore, where achievement motive aims to maximize satisfaction of some kind, the aim of avoidance motive is to minimize pain by avoiding pain giving situation.

The persons having a greater degree of achievement motive or avoidance motive are found to have a peculiar level of aspiration. While the person having avoidance motive will either not like to take any task in hand or will choose most simple and easy task or will choose most difficult task where there is no chance for success. Thereby he chooses such activities which minimize his anxiety about failure. On the other hand, the person in whom the achievement motive is stronger is found to set his level of aspiration in the intermediate zone where there is moderate risk. Further, when free to choose, such person always looks for new and more difficult task as he masters old problem. In this way, the person, who is more motivated to achieve, tries to maximize his own anxiety about failure, struggle hard for getting success and derive maximum pleasure from success.

## Characteristics of the persons having high achievement motivation

1. The level of aspiration of such people is found to be higher. But they raise it step by step and always set in it the intermediate zone where there is moderate risk.
2. They show greater persistence in work at an achievement related task.
3. They are found to derive more pleasure from success than the people who are weak in achievement motive.
4. They show more efficiency or a higher level of accomplishment.
5. There is strong desire to excel and beat others or to perform the best and shine in material terms, among such persons.
6. They are found to possess more anxiety about getting success in comparison to the people who are weak in achievement motive.
7. Persons having materialistic attitude, belong to higher caste and capitalistic strata, are found to possess strong achievement motive.

McClelland (1965) prepared a list of various propositions and conditions for developing achievement motivation, some of which are described below:

1. *Reasons to develop a motive:* The individual should have in advance many reasons to believe that he should develop an achievement motive.
2. *Realistic and reasonable motive:* The individual should understand that this motive is realistic and reasonable.
3. *Clearly understanding and describing various aspects of the motive:* The individual should be able to clearly understand and describe various aspects of the achievement motive.
4. *Linking the motive to related actions and deeds:* The individual should be able to link the motive to related actions and deeds in order to bring about change in thoughts and actions.
5. *Linking the motive to events:* If the individual is able to link the achievement motive to events in his day-to-day life, his thoughts and actions will be influenced by achievement motivation.
6. *Seeing the motive as an improvement in self-image:* The thoughts and actions of the individual will be influenced by the achievement motive when the individual sees the motive as an improvement in his self image.
7. *Self commitment to achievement of concrete goals in life:* The individual should be able to achieve concrete goals in life related to the achievement motive.
8. *Keeping a record of progress towards achieving committed goals:* Individual should keep a record of his progress towards achieving goals by which he is committed.
9. *Warm feeling and honest support and respect by others:* It is likely that changes in motives occur in an atmosphere where the person feels warmly but honestly supported and in which others respect him as an individual capable of guiding and directing his own behaviour in the future.

10. *Significance of self-study:* The setting should dramatize the significance of self-study and lift it out of the routine of everyday life. This will increase the probability of more changes in motive.

11. *Achievement as a sign of membership in a new reference group:* There is likelihood of occurrence of changes in motives if the achievement is a sign of membership in a new reference group.

It is the duty of the educator to help the student lacking the desire to achieve to acquire the desire or the motive.

## Achievement Motivation and Teacher

In the role of a manager of learning activities, the teacher's role is not only to assemble materials, organize them into viable units and draw up programmes and plans for putting them across his students, but he has also to devise strategies and tactics by which students may be persuaded to put their best foot forward and apply themselves wholeheartedly to the tasks he has assigned them in such a manner that they assume responsibility for their achievement and to arouse and encourage them to continue pursuing their learning goals effectively. Most of the students who join college do so with the explicit object of learning and achieving certain goals. The teacher's task is to clarify these goals for both students and their parents and then try to arouse their interest in their pursuit.

The common Indian practice is to make students learn and achieve through one or the other form of correction, physical punishment or fear of failure. There is hardly any tradition of stimulating students who are not interested and at the best the indifferent students are tactically ignored. Even those who do encourage and stimulate their students and succeed in motivating learning and achievement in class work are not conscious of what they are doing.

Most teachers motivate students by holding periodical tests, examinations at the end of every term, awarding marks and prizes, passing judgements of 'pass', offering temptations of a prize or scholarship or inducing fear of failure. These are some of the types of pressures which teachers use to drive students to work hard and harder to achieve better. Tests and examinations should serve as useful tools to students for self-evaluation and to teachers for assessing achievement and learning, but too often they are used to produce and intensify anxiety among students. Pressure is mounted every day as examinations draw near, fear of failure among students of average rank creates undue stress and tension and often has a very harmful effect on academic achievement and on their performance. Several studies have been made on the facilitating and debilitating effects of anxiety state in a classroom climate and it has been found that students with aptitude and intellectual ability are less prone to anxiety. It is clear that anxiety when aroused in an examination has a debilitating effect on a student's performance. Some good students too report that they get upset and do less well in examinations, that the more important the examination the less well they do and that even if they know the answers they are unable to get started because of anxiety and do worse than they should. Besides, such a pressure on students is produced; anxiety is bound to spoil teacher-student relations. Corrective measures often have the opposite effect of killing initiative and student's sense of responsibility. They are keen only to carry out the commands of the teacher and make no effort at self direction and self achievement. Their attempts are generally along the lines laid down by the teacher and their main concern is to escape the censure of the teacher.

Some teachers motivate their students by insisting on expectancies. They keep repeating that students attend the college to learn and achieve what is prescribed for them.

They keep giving the advice and directions regarding the tasks to be accomplished and they expect students to comply. As their approach is always of hope and confidence, they do succeed in motivating young people. Most of the teachers who succeed are otherwise effective and students respect their wishes. The total effect on students is the strong feeling that both teachers and students are engaged in tasks which are worthwhile and of vital importance.

Several studies reveal that by far the most effective approach in reinforcing achievement motive is to make the accomplishment of tasks satisfying and pleasant. Whatever may be the difficulty, however hard may be the task, if students enjoy doing it, if their experience is interesting and they expect to succeed, they will learn and achieve. Such teachers rely mostly on praise and recognition by awarding higher marks, giving special concessions and recognition and seeking the support of parents and too often they succeed. Most of the psychological researches lend support to the views that rewards are more effective than punishments. Rewarding correct learning increases the prospect of its recurrence as has been indicated in a class in which the social and emotional climate is healthy, mere completion of work in a group makes for strong motivation for achievement.

Happy interpersonal relations between the teacher and students are a strong motivating force in achievement. Where the teacher and students are happy with each other, where the teacher has a deep interest in the welfare of his students and where both have confidence in each other's good will, affection and friendship, the students will always be on the look-out to please and win the approval and recommendation of the teacher, to live and work up to his expectation and to enjoy doing what is expected of them. The teacher from his part must see that the tasks allotted to students are well within their capacity, that he himself not only feels but also shows himself involved in student's efforts and activities.

## Achievement Motivation and Students

The process of learning is in favour of the teacher. Students attend the college to learn and achieve things and to make learning and achievement effective, the teacher has to appeal to the pre-existing needs, desires, interests and motives of students. Psychologists commonly agree that these physiological and psychological needs do motivate behaviour, learning and achievement and the teacher cannot afford to neglect them. But, then he has to create, induce and strengthen new needs, interests and motives and these needs must be based on pre-existing needs, interests and motives.

In colleges, curricular requirements and teaching loads are so heavy that the teacher sets the goals and pressurizes students to achieve them within a prescribed period of time. He motivates students by expectations, demands or other types of coercive as have been described. Tasks are given every day and students complete them as they are expected to, without seeing the meaning and purpose, merit and value of what they have done. The responsibility and initiative belongs to the teacher and the students have just to comply. They may see goals of the specific assignments by completing every day or week but not the overall goal which encompasses the smaller ones. Motivation in such an arrangement can be high, but often the teacher depending entirely on obedience and compliance has to fall back upon other crutches like rewards, punishments and pressures. There is a danger that students may weaken or falten in their effort because they do not see what this is all about. Fortunately, most students in India come from homes for which collegeing is a passage to improvement in social status, employment and material advantage in life, and they give themselves up into the hands of the teacher and carry out his behest. But, if real education is self-education, if students' perceptions and experiences are more important than those of the teacher, and if they have to develop initiative, self-direction and self-reliance, the goals they strive for most be chosen by them and not imposed on them by the teacher. The teacher's help and guidance will always be needed but he should lay before them a number of alternatives and possibilities from which they make their choice. Often, students will want to know more about a topic. Before committing himself, the teacher should be ready with suggestions for further reading and inquiry. Sometimes, they may not be clear about the value of any goal and may be attracted by some superficial aspect. The teacher may clarify. He may also provide opportunity for group discussion in which several members of the class participate and analyse different alternatives and plans.

This method will be more effective with college students than with school pupils, partly because the grown-ups develop self-reliance and wish to do without the help of the teacher, and partly because at the college level there are several streams of studies and courses and students are obliged to make a choice. Since this choice between humanities, science, computers, technology, commerce, management, agriculture, arts, etc., is going to make a difference to their later life and to the whims and fancies of parents or teachers. Of course, students do not understand the pros and cons of the several professions and careers to which a particular course will lead, but it is important and necessary to discuss goals with students and let them make the choice. In doing so, they may have to be told about their aptitudes and abilities, their capacity or otherwise to undertake a particular course, but ultimately the choice should be theirs. When goals are their own, the college work will seem more meaningful and worthwhile and no effort will be spared to do well.

There will be many students to whom the goal of preparing for life, a career or a profession does not hold any appeal. They are too much concerned with the present, dawdling, seeing films or matches, gossiping and even feeling proud of neglecting their studies. A helpful remedy for such students will be provided by the new movement in Indian education for providing 'work experience' to students.

Teachers will certainly say that with crowded curricula and a limited period of time within which to cover courses, it is very difficult for them to let students take the initiative, particularly when examination results are going to affect their annual promotion. They, therefore, opt for the short-cut route of laying down clearly what is to be learned and putting students through the paces to learn it. This difficulty of teachers is quite understandable, but no less understandable is the truth that young people learn best by what they themselves do and experience. Behaviour and movements induced from outside by the teacher may not have any meaning for the student.

In helping students to select their own goals, the resourcefulness of the teacher will be put to a severe test. He must have a rich and varied acquaintance with a large variety of people in history, fiction, biography and current life so as to be able to present several models and pictures of life and work, from the world of music, sports, entertainment, industry, science and literature so that students choose the kind of idols they should identify themselves with.

When students share in the information of goals, these goals can be used as a feedback. If the goals are stated by the teacher or a group of students in the class, feedback is involved in discussing the extent to which students clearly understand and accept them. When students understand their goals clearly, they will be able to gauge their progress towards the goals and this knowledge of their progress is an extremely effective form of motivation. Feedback will provide a clear insight into the meaning of goals. Praise is one of the most readily available methods of keeping students informed of their progress. By gestures and words, a teacher can convey his approval or commendation and they act as an effective feedback for students. Even criticism is better than being utterly ignored. At least the criticized student will feel that he does matter in the class.

## Achievement Motivation and Self-Concept

Self-concept is the individual's perception of his abilities and his status and roles in the outer world is called the self-concept. Current educational literature implies that a learner who has a suitable self-concept will learn more easily in school situation than one who has an inappropriate self-concept. It is frequently argued that a person who thinks himself stupid is likely to be more poorly motivated in an academic learning situation than a person who thinks himself bright. It is assumed that there is a causal relation between the self-concept and the rate of learning and achievement. But some researches show that it may be the other way round, the high quality of achievement may be the cause of superior self-concept.

There is another dimension of self-concept, which is very important from the point of view of achievement motivation. The self-concept also refers to the ideal self too, that is, the kind of person the individual aspires to be. While there is no reliable evidence as to the exact nature of the motivational influence which the ideal self-concept exercises on a student's achievement, one study has revealed that those students who had shown greater discrepancy between ideal self and self-concept showed a high degree of achievement motivation. Why this is so, the research study was unable to indicate. The ideal self and the concept of self were rated on a set of traits commonly believed to be related to achievement.

One thing is clear that the ideal self is related to what is called the level of aspiration, which is the level of future performance on a familiar task which an individual expects to reach. The expectation is defined in terms of the level the individual says he will perform on the task. Success will mean that he has surpassed the level he expects to reach, and failure is the reverse. Since success and failure are relative to the level of aspiration and are great reinforcing forces in learning and achievement, the self-concept and the level of aspiration are great motivational forces for learning and achievement. A pupil's self-concept will decide what goals suit him and how he should strive for their realization, and it will also determine his level of aspiration. The more he expects of himself, that is, the higher his level of aspiration, the more effort he will put into achieving the task. The level of aspiration and the self-image change with the degree and extent of achievement and are susceptible to change by success. Failure seems to have less effect because it spurs some people to try harder, rather than lower the level of aspiration. In some cases, failure does lower the level of aspiration. Students who fail to achieve their goal often show a tendency to lower their level of aspiration in subsequent situations. Failure generates a state of anxiety and success fill one with hope, and both are strong influences on achievement.

Students differ in their self-image and levels of aspiration. Some place their expectations too high, others put them low and quite a few are very realistic in their expectations. So, the relation of self-concept and level of aspiration to achievement motivation is complex. Several studies made show that there is no direct correlation between the level of aspiration and achievement motivation but it was found that students who had a strong achievement motivation and were anxious about success in a stressful achievement situation have a lower level of aspiration than other students.

However, the self-concept does make a difference to learning and achievement. A student who sees himself as a machine man in his father's factory three years hence cannot see any good in the learning of geography or algebra. For enlisting achievement motivation, the teacher must know something about the students' ambitions and aspirations, how they perceive themselves and what they hope to become in life. But in a general way, it may be said that all young people wish to feel adequate, to be admired and praised, to be considered capable and competent, to have a status in their group and to win self-esteem. It is for the teacher to devise situation in the classroom in such a manner that these feeling of esteem, adequacy and status depend on high achievement and a high level of aspiration is set consistent with the capabilities of students. Young people are generally eager for self-enhancement, they not only wish to be well spoken of but also are eager to work hard to achieve a position of respect among their classmates, and it is clearly the responsibility of the teacher that he should in cooperation with parents try to understand their aspirations and help and encourage them to realize them. Achievement motivation will spring from such needs and aspirations.

## Achievement Motivation and Social Factors

Classroom climate, competition and cooperation and the role of the teacher in classroom activity and work have already been dealt with, as also their contribution to achievement motivation. In so far as the worth and esteem of a student depends largely on the reactions and evaluations of his classmates, the peer group or the class is an important factor in achievement motivation. It is a common experience that a young person is more sensitive to the opinions and demands of his classmates than those of his teachers or parents, and his self-concept is largely influenced by them. Very often the classroom climate, the norms and code prevailing in the class, determine the responses that student make to the teacher's solicitations and questions. They may help or obstruct learning. Usually, the teacher dominates the class by setting tasks and instilling a spirit of competition among students, and the desire to excel and distinguish over-rides group inhibitions, if any. This is frequently seen even in colleges where every effort is made to soften the excitement of competition.

Young students often identify themselves with one another, they love to be like their close friends. In some classes, there is great cohesiveness and group tasks are set, units of work are undertaken by small groups within the class and a spirit of give-and-take prevails. But, there is a danger in such a pattern of achievement motivation. The achievements of the class remain at the mediocre level. Outstanding achievement by individual students is facilitated by rivalry and competition, but then if one student scores very high, it makes the rest look bad, and an element of conflict mars the atmosphere of the class. If some students always top the class in every subject and activity, it is a great damper for the rest. So, the teacher must see that a happy balance is maintained between the high and the low in the matter of attention, encouragement and stimulation.

But the classroom climate cannot remain unaffected by the atmosphere prevailing in the college. The motto of the college, the reputation it has made in the local community, the distinctions in public examinations and tournaments of its former alumni and the way they are given prominence in the college, the values and ideals which the college cherishes, publicizes and expects its students to cultivate and follow, all these bear on the achievement motivation of students, and the classroom work cannot possibly remain unaffected by them.

## Achievement Motivation and Examination

Examination success has always been used to motivate learning and achievement. Most parents and their wards look to examination success as the main aim of their educational effort, for the government and private agencies of employment set much store by examination results, and the teacher, hedged in by top-heavy syllabi and limited time, seldom fails to exploit this need for motivating his students for better and greater learning and achievement.

There is a hard core of educationists who attack examinations vehemently, but the vast majority of teacher's value examinations for their potential for achievement motivation. It is difficult to imagine how it is possible to do without examinations, for in a society, people are constantly assessing each other and motivate one another in terms of such assessments, however diversely made. The most important thing is not to abolish examinations but to reduce the ill-effects of the prevailing examination system so that students are motivated to achieve worthwhile things. Some of the reforms called for are:

1. Reducing the emotional strain and tension which accompany examinations;
2. Introducing more varied kinds of examinations;
3. Providing more opportunities for reassessment; and
4. Placing greater emphasis on activities disassociated from competitive examinations.

## Achievement Motivation and Parents

Students of achievement motivation show many factors at work and among them are parental attitudes. It is obvious that achievement motivation tends to be high when parents have high aspirations for themselves, when their own achievements are noteworthy and when they stress and expect independence, excellence and high achievement from their children. Young people frequently tend to identify themselves with their successful parents and try to emulate their example. Dominant and demanding parents, however, tend to overwhelm them and they avoid involvement in tasks.

## Achievement Motivation and Anxiety

The field of motivation is still uncharted and several studies and researches in this field have not yet produced a complete picture from which the subject may be clearly and adequately understood. What has been presented here is a fragmentary discussion of what things have come to light. Our knowledge of anxiety and hope as accompaniments of achievement motivation are not adequate and await further study and investigation.

Anxiety is not a pleasant state of feeling and our present knowledge of anxiety is derived from clinical studies of abnormal people who manifest extremely intense anxiety and also of those people who have no anxiety at all. Such disturbed people perform some compulsive acts for the purpose of reducing their anxiety. Mental disturbance causes anxiety and those compulsive acts restore order and reduce anxiety. Such studies have rejected mild anxiety which all normal people feel and often love to feel. It may be a pleasurable experience if so many people seek pursuits which involve anxiety adventurer, the amateur gambler, card and chess players, seek experiences which ban anxiety and others spend money and time to get these exhilarating experiences.

Experiments with anxiety are difficult, but one research has shown that in the learning of very simple responses like a simple conditioned reflex, there is greater speed in the learning of people with high anxiety than in the learning of low anxiety people. So, anxiety works as a motive. But, in learning complex tasks, high anxiety results in confused responses. In training people for emergent situations of high anxiety, like the training of air pilots, highly over-learned responses must be ensured so that in high anxiety emergency, only correct responses are made. But, in ordinary classroom situations, only mild anxiety is capable of functioning as an achievement motive, too high anxiety leads to confused responses and too low anxiety is ignored. Hope leads to exploratory behaviour and is a positive reinforcement for achievement.

Therefore, the teacher may produce a little anxiety among pupils when he is teaching familiar and easy tasks, taking care not to increase it beyond the mild state. Hope and confidence, however, are more productive.

## Inducing Achievement Motivation

Kurt Lewin distinguished between inner and induced motivation and Lippit and White in their classic experiment studied the effects of different leadership styles in children's tendency to develop their own motivation with regard to group achievement. In authoritarian leadership, when policy is determined and dictated by the leaders, and evaluation is personal and arbitrary, students developed little of their own motivation. They worked productively when the leader was present but the lack of personal motivation was shown in reduction in productivity and increase in aggression when the leader left the room, absence of motivation when the leader arrived late, negligence in work, lack of initiative in offering spontaneous suggestions, lack of pride in the products of the group effort. But, under democratic leadership, group discussion and decision were encouraged, students depended less on the leader, they went on working even when he was absent or late. Unity of work made them happy. They selected their own goals, they created their own forces towards the goal and achievement motivation was high.

In inducing achievement motivation among students, various psychological processes are involved and these processes are inter-related. The first step is that of creating a particular cognitive structure. A person's behaviour is guided by his perception of the world in which he lives. Action is taken on the basis of a person's view of the 'facts' of the situation and the facts are coloured by his beliefs and opinions, the private map, in order to say that he maintains the world. The content and relationships among parts of a person's psychological world may be called his cognitive structure. Since this structure underlies all behaviour efforts to influence a student, behaviour will succeed only if this structure undergoes a change.

The first task of the teacher is to make young people understand very clearly why they have come to college for, what are the aims and objectives of course work, what is the programme for class work in this term or month and what is expected of them. This knowledge and understanding will re-orient them cognitively to college work. Many students come to college because their parents want them to get out of their way. They do not care what their wards learn or do not learn and naturally, for such students the college may not be a place for learning and achievement. On the other hand, there are students whose parents send them to college with the express intent that they learn and achieve things and this intent is very clearly dinned into their ears. The understanding, opinions and thoughts of the latter will incline them more to accept the messages of the teacher because they are consistent with their cognitive structure.

The second step is the creation of a motivational structure which means the teacher must create in the minds of students, the needs, the interests and purposes which will energize learning and achieving behaviour. If the teacher suggests to them, to choose the goal and if they are persuaded to accept them as worthwhile and vital, they will work for their achievement and fulfillment.

The needs of hunger and thirst are accompanied by a discomfort which energizes action but the motive for achievement does not carry with it any insistent prod within any clear limitation of time. Therefore, the teacher must see that achievement motivation gains control of student's behaviour at a particular point of time. This is the third step of creating behaviour structure in the process of induction of motive. The teacher will have to keep other motive out of focus and assign specific tasks to be completed at a particular point in time the goal and tasks should be concrete and specific and if a time limit is given for their fulfillment and completion, it will precipitate learning activity and achievement.

## Academic Achievement

According to Webster's third Micro International Dictionary (1961), achievement means 'the capacity to achieve the desired results'.

In the Oxford English Dictionary, it has the meaning: 'The accomplishment, execution, carrying out, working out of anyting ordered or undertaken, the doing of any action or work'. 'Something performed or done, an action in emphatic sense, a notable deed, achievement'.

The term academic achievement is a very broad term, which indicates generally the learning outcome of students. Achievement of these learning outcomes requires a series of planned and organized experiences and hence learning is called a process. In this process of achievement of change in behaviour, one cannot say that all students reach the same level of change during the same span of time. The level of achievement reached by the students is called the academic achievement of students.

Learning affects three major areas of behaviour of students: cognitive, affective, and psychomotor, respectively. It is difficult to say without proper evidence, that the students reach the same level in all the three domains at a time. Students may be at a somewhat higher level in one domain and at a somewhat lower level in other domain. This means that students may be at different levels of achievement in different areas. As the areas of affective domain and psychomotor domain are not sufficiently explored, it is generally a custom to restrict the term 'college performance' to the level of achievement of students in the cognitive areas of various college subjects. Here, one should not restrict oneself to only academic performances but also to the accomplishments in other areas. In order to find out the academic achievement of students, evaluation is necessary.

Evaluation is an integral part of the teaching-learning process and it involves identifying and defining instructional objectives in behavioural terms, using suitable learning experiences, and constructing suitable evaluation instruments and appraising various learning outcomes.

Virtually, all the teachers use some kind of tests to evaluate the progress of their students. Here are some of the principles of measurement of educational achievement as given by Robert Ebel (1971).

1. The measurement of educational achievement is essential to evaluate effective education.
2. An educational test is no more or less than a devise for facilitating, extending and refining a teacher's observation of students' achievement.
3. Every important outcome of education can be a measurement.
4. The most important educational achievement is command of useful knowledge.
5. Written tests are well suited to measure the student's command of useful knowledge.

There are many students who pass the examination, yet they fail to achieve as much as they can in terms of their abilities. These students are known as under-achievers. They are the persons who are quite capable, but fail to achieve in conformity with their capacities for several reasons. Perhaps, certain non-intellectual factors may interfere with their achievement.

An important need in the prediction of academic achievement is systematic research into personality characteristics and academic motivation which are conducive to academic achievement.

**Factors Affecting Achievement**

Achievement is a function of personal as well as environmental factors, individuals tend to mainly attribute their behaviour or level of performance ·more to one than the other of these two factors. Applied to education, it is an attempt to explain individual differences as the causes of their failures and successes in academic task and the effects of such beliefs. (Weiner, et. al., 1971).

Attributions in terms of personal and impersonal causes are everyday occurrences. Ability is considered as relatively a stable individual trait. Task easiness is a stable factor which is not within the student's control and luck is an unstable factor. Weiner and his colleagues (1971) analysed causal attribution in terms of these four factors: ability, effort, task difficulty and luck. On one hand, ability and efforts are considered personal or internal while task difficulty and luck are impersonal or external; and on the other, ability and task difficulty are considered stable while effort and luck are unstable factors.

Achievement is the performance of the student's accomplishment in a subject. Study of achievement with some of its correlates has become a topic of key interest among the researchers today. Academic achievement depends on a number of variables. Important among them are the students' socio-economic status and their achievement motivation.

Educational cpportunities, through open to all, do not seem to engage to any reasonable extent the capacities of those who seek to avail themselves of them. An eternal question baffling parents, educators and planers is: why do students of demonstrated ability flop in their academic efforts at school or college examination?

Academic underachievement, more than academic failure, constitutes a grave problem as it amounts to wastage of human resources which is construed as an irreparable loss to the society, which a developing country like India can ill-afford. This stimulated a number of researchers to undertake studies, like the present study, on academic achievement. There are a number of researches on achievement and the factors that are influencing the achievement of students. Achievement is influenced by many factors like values, intelligence, creativity, socio-economic status, the level of aspiration, etc.

Taylor (1964) stated that the value the student places upon his own worth, effects his academic achievement. Very low level of expectation tends to make a student accept very low standard of achievement, very high expectation leads to discouragement and diminished effort because he feels he cannot live up to what is required of him. To be practical, the level of expectation needs to be general to suit to each individual's capability.

Academic achievement, as excellence in all academic disciplines, includes excellence in sporting, behaviour, confidence, communication skills, punctuality, assertiveness, arts, culture, and the like. Academic performance refers to how students deal with their studies and how they cope with or accomplish different tasks given to them by their teachers. Academic performance is the ability to study and remember facts and being able to communicate your knowledge verbally or down on paper.

## Alcoholism

The term alcohol consumption encompasses two ideas important in characterizing an individual's drinking behaviour: frequency (how often a person drinks) and quantity (how much a person drinks). Frequency of consumption refers to the number of days or, sometimes, occasions that an individual has consumed alcoholic beverages during a specified interval (e.g., week, month and year). Quantity of consumption refers to the amount ingested on a given drinking occasion.

In human individual, adolescent-onset alcohol abuse has been associated with a reduction in the size of the hippocampus. Research also suggests that adolescents are less sensitive than adults to some of the alcoholic effects. Numerous other factors affect drinking behaviour among college students. These include biological and genetic predisposition to use, belief system and personality, and expectations about the effects of alcohol (Sher, et.al., 1999; Zucker, et. al., 1995). In addition to individual student characteristics, the size of a student body, geographical location, and importance of athletics on campus are also associated with consumption patterns as are external environmental variables including the pricing and availability of alcohol in the area surrounding a campus. The prevalence of periodic heavy or high-risk drinking is greatest among young adults aged 19 to 24; and among young adults, college students have the highest prevalence of high-risk drinking.

Drinking behaviour is complex, and there is need to broaden the range of issues studied, particularly extending analysis to the economic, political and ecological factors that have thus far received far less study than the psycho-social issues. Previous studies stated that currently 1.9 million young people between the ages of 12 and 20 are considered heavy drinkers and 4.4 million are binge drinkers. Young people at highest risk for early drinking are those with a history of abuse, family violence, depression and stressful life events. People with a family history of alcoholism are also more likely to begin drinking before the age of 20 and to become alcoholic. A survey of 5000 adults over 60 years of age reported that 15 per cent of men and 12 per cent of women were hazardous drinkers, and 9 per cent of men and 3 per cent of women were alcohol dependent. Most alcoholics are men, but the incidence of alcoholism in women has been increasing over the past 30 years. About 9.3 per cent of women are heavy drinkers and 22.8 per cent of men are binge drinkers compared to 8.7 per cent of women. Severely depressed or anxious people are at high risk for alcoholism, smoking and other forms of addiction. Social phobia causes an intense fear of being publicly scrutinized and humiliated. Such individuals may use alcohol as a way to become less inhibited in public situations. Although 54 per cent of urban adults use alcohol at least once a month compared to 42 per cent in non-urban areas, living in the city or the country does not affect the risks for bingeing or heavy alcohol use. People who carve sugar may also be at higher risk for alcoholism.

The Research Society on Alcoholism (RSA) in USA provides a forum for communication among researchers who share common interests in alcoholism. The society's purpose is to promote research that can lead the way toward prevention and treatment of alcoholism. The RSA (established in 1976) assists and encourages the application of research to the solution of problems related to alcoholism and also serves as a meeting ground for scientists working in all fields of alcoholism and alcohol related problems.

Commitments are needed from the community surrounding the college campus, as well as from funding sources such as foundations, national organizations, and the hospitality and alcohol beverage industries to support only comprehensive, research based strategies for addressing underage and excessive college drinking. Strategies are clearly needed to engage these students as early as possible in appropriate screening and intervention services — whether provide on campus or through referral to specialized community based services, one important effort to increase on-campus screening services.

Norms or values clarification examines students' perceptions about the acceptability of abusive drinking behaviour and uses data to refute beliefs about the tolerance for this behaviour as well as beliefs about the number of students who drink excessively and the amounts of alcohol they consume. Motivational enhancement is designed to stimulate students' intrinsic desire or motivation to change their behaviour. Motivational enhancement strategies are based on the theory that individuals alone are responsible for changing their drinking behaviour and complying with that decision.

The programme, the Alcohol Skills Training Program (ASTP), is a cognitive behavioural alcohol prevention programme in USA that teaches students basic principles of moderate drinking and how to cope with high-risk situations for excessive alcohol consumption. To address these serious consequences of alcohol consumption by college students, the National Advisory Council to the National Institute on Alcohol Abuse and Alcoholism (NIAAA) established the Task Force on College Drinking in 1998. The composition of the Task Force was novel in USA. College presidents and research scientists were put together to ensure that the product would at the same time contribute to the scientific basis for addressing college drinking and would be relevant to the practical challenges faced by college administrators. The Task Force was charged with integrating available scientific research with experiences reported by administrators, service providers and students.

Thus, the culture of drinking is antithetical to the culture of learning, which is the core of higher education. It threatens the health and safety of all students, disrupts the academic process, frustrates faculty, and disturbs the lives of those in adjacent communities. So, campus based task forces have to direct prevention programme efforts and develop specific strategies for promoting change in student organizations.

**Effects of Alcohol Centre**

| Medical Problem | Light-Moderate Drinking | Binge Drinking and Hangovers | Heavy Chronic Drinking |
|---|---|---|---|
| 1 | 2 | 3 | 4 |
| Liver Disorders | | Change in liver function | Alcoholic Hepatitis, Cirrhosis |
| Gastrointestinal Problems | | Diarrhoea | Diarrhoea. Hemorrhoids. Pencreatitis. Bleeding in the intestines and stomach. Tears in the esophagus from violent vomiting. |
| Heart Disease | *Beneficial:* May help reduce risk for heart disease caused by blockage of arteries | High Blood pressure. Increased heart rate. Heart rhythm disturbances. | High Blood Pressure weakened heart muscles leading to failure |
| Stroke | *Beneficial:* May help reduce risk for ischemic stroke (strokes caused by blockage in the arteries to the brain) | | Hemorrhagic Stroke |

*(Contd...)*

| 1 | 2 | 3 | 4 |
|---|---|---|---|
| Cancer | Associated with higher risk for breast cancer in women | | Cancers in the head and neck, esophagus, stomach, liver pancreas, and cervix and vagina (in women). (Effect of heavy drinking on breast cancer is unclear) |
| Neurological or Mental Disorders | Insomnia Headache | Memory Impairment and problems in thinking and concentration | Nerve damage from severe vitamin deficiencies. Impairment in mental functioning and memory. Emotional disorders, psychosis |
| Genital and (Reproductive) | Increase sexual drive (although even modest drinking can cause importance in men). Even moderate drinking during pregnancy increases risk for birth defects. | Any drinking during pregnancy increases risk for birth defects. | Importance in Men. Menstrual disorders and infertility in women. Drinking during pregnancy increases risk for birth defects |

(Contd...)

| 1 | 2 | 3 | 4 |
|---|---|---|---|
| Immune System | | | Increased susceptibility to infections |
| (Skin, Muscle, and Bone Disorders) | | | Osteoporosis Muscular Deterioration Skin sores. Itching Peripheral neuropathy |
| Diabetes | Possibly beneficial, though associated with hypoglycemia | Hypoglycemia | Hypoglycemia |
| Lung Disorders | | | Acute respiratory Distress Syndrome Pneumonia |

One needs to keep himself/herself away from alcohol after noticing the ill-effects of alcoholism.

Awareness of alcohol use and misuse is not new. Anecdotal reports indicate that approximately 80 per cent of college students drink and that half of the college student drinkers engage in heavy episodic drinking. Excessive alcohol intake among college students is associated with a variety of adverse consequences: fatal and non-fatal injuries, alcohol poisoning, blackouts, academic failure, violence including rape and assault, unintended pregnancy, sexually transmitted diseases including HIV/AIDS, and property damage. Students who engage in excessive drinking impact not just themselves, fellow students experience second-hand consequences ranging from disrupted study and sleep to physical and sexual assault.

## RESEARCH STUDIES

As this study intends to find out the level of the achievement motivation and academic achievement of alcoholic and non-alcoholic college students, let us look into the findings of the previous studies related to these aspects.

### Academic Achievement

The following are some of the studies related to academic achievement.

### Academic Achievement and Adjustment

Desai (1979) and Hirunval (1980) reported a positive relationship between class room climate and pupils' academic achievement.

Nagpal (1979) observed that the under-achievers reported a greater number of adjustment problems and more academic adjustment problems. The high-achievers were well adjusted with family and were also better adjustment personality than the under-achievers.

Reddy (1978) found that adjustment has significantly related to scholastic performance. Among other results, it is of significance to note that the attitude to self, learning, achievement, parents, teachers and peers were found to be positively related to academic adjustment and scholastic performance.

Soman (1977) noticed the overlapping of fourteen affective variables belonging to basic personality's dimension of achievement in mathematics. This revealed that personal adjustment variables and anxiety variables had a considerable influence on achievement in mathematics. The dominant personality factor identified for the over-achievers was individual adjustment factor.

Chopra (1988) reported that academic achievement has positive relationship with attitude towards education and also with the study habits of students. Further, home adjustment was found to be more closely related to academic than emotional, health and social adjustment.

## Academic Achievement and Gender

Bhatttacaryya, Anjana (1989) reported that boys performed better than girls on verbal reasoning test. In abstract reasoning test, boys showed superiority over girls.

Menon (1972) identified that job aspiration, educational aspiration and general ambition were strongly associated with high achievement in girls.

Patel (1977) observed no significant difference in the achievement between urban boys and urban girls; but in case of rural areas, girls were superior to boys.

Patil, I. (1982) found no significant difference in the n-achievement of superior and average boys.

## Academic Achievement and Home Background

Chatterji, et. al. (1971) investigated the effect of parent's education, family size and general condition of the home upon scholastic achievement. The family size and the number of siblings were inversely related to the scholastic achievement especially in the low intellectual level. Parents' help has significant positive contribution towards higher achievement; and parents' educational level was directly related to the achievement of their children. But, father's occupation did not show considerable effect. However, the study conclusively demonstrated that parent's education has related to scholastic achievement.

Chopra (1988) reported that the students' home and health attitude towards education were figured as some of the non-intellectual correlates of academic achievement.

Pyari (1980) observed that the relationship between family attachment scores and educational achievement scores was found to be negatively significant.

Salunke (1979) reported that educational facilities and emotional happiness in home contributed positively to the pupils' performance.

## Academic Achievement and Inelligence

Acharyulu (1978), while studying interactive effects of creativity on achievement, found that intelligence has positive effect on academic achievement. Menon (1980) has also found the same results.

Alegaokar (1981) noticed that high achievers in physical achievement had higher I.Q. than low achievers. High achievers in jump and reach, as well as those in long jump and ball throw, had higher I.Q. than low achievers.

Aruna, N.S. (1981) identified a significant correlation of 0.44 between intelligence and academic achievement of SC and ST students.

Burwani, Rupa G. (1991) found that intellectual competence had high positive influence upon academic achievement of both science group and commerce group. Academic achievement was positively associated with intellectual competence.

Chatterji, P.S. (1983) noticed that science students were more intelligent than arts students. Science students achieved significantly higher verbal factor and total intelligence scores than others and they were significantly superior in numerical factor of intelligence in comparison with arts and science students. Scores on intelligence test in science group were significantly higher than others.

Chaudhary, N. (1971) found correlation between n-achievement and intelligence scores for the combined samples and for the boys were not significant, whereas the same was significant at 0.01 level for girls.

Dhall, Taruna C. and Salni, Madhu (2008) found that children of working mothers having similar intelligence, receiving high cognitive stimulation exhibited higher academic performance as compared to those receiving low cognitive stimulation. Children of non-working mothers having similar intelligence, receiving high cognitive stimulation were found to exhibit higher academic performance as compared to those receiving low cognitive stimulation.

George (1966) revealed that the pupils with high intelligence and higher achievers had better adjustment.

Jogi, J.K. (1984) found that intelligence had a significant effect on the achievement.

Kabu (1980) investigated the factor of intelligence and was found to have significant influence on mathematical talent at the under-graduate level.

Kumari, Indira (1990) found that children with high intelligence achieved conservation of mass, weight and volume easier than those who were of low intelligence.

Manoranjan, Panda (2005) found a significant difference in academic achievement of students studying in different categories of schools. There is a low relationship between academic achievement and intelligence in different categories of schools.

Mehta, P. and others (1967) found that n-achievement has a positive correlation with intelligence.

Menon (1980) found that intelligence has a positive effect on academic achievement.

Mukharji (1970) found that intelligence has a significant positive influence on scholastic achievement.

Sharma, K.L. (1978) noticed that achievement showed highest relationship with intelligence.

Sunil Kiran, K.S. (2005) found the influence of emotional intelligence on academic achievement.

Vidhu, M. (1968) noticed that the correlation between intelligence and academic performance was positive and highly significant.

Zacharia (1977) found that the pupils' intelligence was a major factor in influencing their achievement in Social Studies and observed that pupils' attitude and intelligence scores were more or less equally correlated with their achievement in Social Studies.

**Academic Achievement and Locality**

Bhatttacaryya, Anjana (1989) found that urban students performed better than rural students on verbal reasoning test. Rural boys performed better than rural girls. Urban girls showed superiority over rural girls.

**Academic Achievement and Personality**

Abraham, P.A. (1969) reported the influence of the temperamental dimensions of neuroticism and introversion-extraversion on academic achievement showed sex differences. Factor analysis of the personality variables and academic achievement evolved a factor pattern in which three factors could be identified, viz. scholastic aptitude, neuroticism and extraversion-introversion.

Acharya, P. (1991) reported that the reflective group of subjects showed superior performance in comparison to the impulsive performance of personality of individuals.

Agarwal (1975) found that under-achievers were comparatively less emotionally mature, less calm, less placed, less prone to getting in to difficulties, less able to face reality, and possessing less ego strength than over-achievers.

Ahuja, Malvinder and Tachanut, Yaiuva (2006) reported that low persistence students achieved equal gain means through Multimedia CAI and CGL (Computer Assisted Instruction and Conventional Group Learning). Average persistence students achieved equal gain means through Multimedia CAI and CGL. High persistence students achieved equal gain mean through Multimedia CAI and CGL. Through Multimedia CAI, high average and low persistence students were found to be equal in their gain means.

Bhargava, K. (1980) reported that academic competence and schizophrenic personality had negative correlation. There was a negative correlation between neuroticism and academic performance.

Burwani, Rupa G. (1991) found that discrepancies between real and ideal self-concept did not affect the academic achievement of commerce group; but in the science group, real and ideal self-concept were positively related. Students who revealed mental ill-health symptoms were poor in academic achievement.

Chatterji, P.S. (1983) reported that scores on the extraversion scale in the commerce group were significantly higher than students in science and arts group; whereas in agriculture group higher than the scores of arts group.

Dhall, Taruna C. and Salni, Madhu (2008) found that working mother's children receiving high cognitive stimulation have better academic performance as compared to those receiving low cognitive stimulation. No significant difference was observed in academic performance scores of elementary school children belonging to moderate and low cognitive stimulation groups.

Ghuman (1976) reported that over-achievers attributed primarily to non-intellective personality variables and under-achievers to intellective factors.

Gupta, Alka (1992) reported that n-achievement, n-affiliation and n-nurturance were positively related.

Hussain (1977) noticed that anxiety found to bear a curvilinear relationship with academic achievement.

Jain (1978) reported that bright achievers were characterized by better study habits and higher achievement motivation than dull achievers.

Jantli, R.T. (1988) reported that neuroticism and extraversion were significantly and negatively related to academic achievement.

Joshi, Renuka (1989) found that the medicine group students scored the lowest on psychoticism and social isolation and the engineering group yielded the highest on these two variables.

Konwar, L.N. (1989) reported that on school socialization the high groups on achievement orientation, general achievement orientation and overall strength showed higher means of personal achievement scores than the low groups.

Koteswara and Ramachandra (2001) reported that all the 14 factors of HSPQ by Cattell's have significant influence on reading achievement of high school students. Students whose personality characteristics were out-going, more intelligent, emotionally stable, excitable, assertive, happy go lucky, super ego strength, venturesome, tense minded, doubting, apprehension, self sufficiency, controlled and tense performed sufficiently better on reading achievement than the students whose personality characteristics were deserved less interested, emotionless, stable, phlegmatic, obedient, jobber, moral, shy, tough-minded, vigorous, placid, group dependent, undisciplined and relaxed.

Kuppuswami (1974) observed that the achievement in school was closely related to the level of aspiration.

Nagpal (1979), Saun (1980), and Patel and Joshi (1977) reported that the under-achievers have social, adjustment, emotional, etc., problems in comparison to over-achievers.

Naik, Ramesh H. (2006) reported that the teachers with introversion orientation will have greater effect on academic achievement of their students in physical science than teachers with extraversion orientation. There was a significant difference between interaction effects of the introversion/extroversion personality type and effective/ineffective teaching on the academic achievement of their students in physical science.

Rao, D.G. (1965) found differences in achievement to be significantly related to aspect of personality like neurotic difficulties, morale and sense of responsibility.

Rao, Venkata (2004) reported a significant difference between the high and low academic achievers with regard to neuroticism. High achievers were more stable than low achievers.

Ravindar (1977) reported that general anxiety by itself had little effect on academic achievement and that combination of anxiety with intelligence considerably increased the accuracy of predicting academic performance.

Saxena, P.C. (1981) studied that a positive self-concept was associated with higher academic achievement in mathematics, commerce and arts streams. The under-achievers were conspicuously of the opposite type, being aware of their actual difficulties and their need for individual help.

Shah (1978) reported that the relationship between self-concept and academic achievement was significantly positive and linear.

Sharma (1979) observed that the level of aspiration did not influence academic achievement.

Sharma, N.K. (1981) reported that neuroticism is not related with academic achievement.

Shukla (1973) reported that the level of aspiration determines the limits of academic achievement to some extent only.

Siddiqui (1979) observed a mutual relationship between intelligence, achievement and personality.

Singh and Kumar (1977) and Bushan and Ahuja (1977) reported that anxiety has a negative relationship with achievement.

Srivastava and Saxena (1979) reported that academically successful students were more extravert than academically unsuccessful students.

Vidhu, M. (1968) reported that extraversion and academic achievement were negatively associated.

**Academic Achievement and Socio-economic Status**

Mehta, P. and others (1967) reported that the high SES school boys showed no relationship between n-achievement and performance.

Satyanandam (1969) found that two sub-aspects of socio-economic status, namely, educational level of parents and economic status of parents have influence on achievement. According to him, the children of graduate parents performed far better than the children of matriculate parents. Children of upper and lower, and upper and middle economic strata only differed significantly on the variable of academic affairs.

Chatterji, et al. (1971) reported that the economic conditions of the family have no effect upon the scholastic achievement in all the intellectual ability groups. Similarly, possession of a study room had no favourable effect in increasing the achievement score in almost all the cases.

Khanna (1980) observed a significant and positive relationship between socio-economic status and academic achievement.

Salunke (1979) reported that socio-economic status was unrelated to academic achievement.

**Academic Achievement and Values**

Agarwal (1975) reported that over-achievers had stronger educational, social and humanistic values than under-achievers.

Pyari (1980) observed that the theoretical, aesthetic, social and religious values were positively and significantly related with educational achievement, while economic and political values were negatively and significantly related.

**Academic Achievement and Drinking**

Hingston, R.W. and Howland, J. (2002) reported that 70,000 students between the ages of 18 and 24 are victims of alcohol related sexual assault or date rape. More than 6,00,000 students between the ages of 18 and 24 are assaulted by another student who has been drinking.

A research analyzed the drinking patterns of 112 college students at a private liberal arts college in USA in which a modified version of the Core Alcohol and Drug Survey was administered. Drinking patterns were determined based on the responses and compared to a measure of academic achievement. 48 per cent of the students who drink alcohol showed patterns consistent with binge drinking (60% male and 40% female). G.P.A. was used as a measure of academic achievement. T-tests were run comparing academic achievement and gender. Women reported having higher G.P.As. than men, both among the entire sample and among bringe drinkers (p=0.028, p=0.032). The mean G.P.A. of males decreased further than the mean G.P.A. of female among students who binge. In a T-test controlled for non-drinkers, intercollegiate athletes drank almost three times as much alcohol per week as non-intercollegiate athletes (M=18.65, M=6.64, p=0.00). In addition, 75 per cent of the athletes reported binge drinking compared to 33 per cent of the non-athletes.

Clapp, J.D. and McDonnell, A.L. (2000) reported that 84 per cent of the students have the habit of drinking during the previous school years.

Dennis Thombs (1991) observed that athlete students are most likely to be at greater risk for alcohol abuse than non-athletes. Heavy consumption rate of the student athletes appeared to exceed that of the university's student body (44.9% and 37.1% respectively).

Jordan Sorenson (1990) observed that parental alcoholism buffers the effects of a child's academic and educational success.

Molstad, S., McMillan, C., Kher, N. and Kilcoyne, M. (1998) reported that college presidents have identified the use and abuse of alcohol by students on campuses as the most significant problem affecting student life.

Lall, R. and Schankler, S.L. (1991) noticed that college students consume greater amounts of alcohol than the general population.

Rakesh Lall (1991) observed that excessive drinking may have detrimental effects on the students academic performance. A student grades may suffer because the time required to academically succeed is being spent pursuing or consuming alcohol.

Schaller, M., Kemeny, A. and Maltzman, I. (1992) reported that few young adults had the ability to remain in good academic standing at a competitive university if a severe dependency on alcohol develops after admission into the college.

Weschsler, H. Kuo, M., and Dowdall, G.W. (2000) observed that 44 per cent of the college students were engaged in binge drinking.

## Achievement Motivation

Some of the studies here under mentioned are related to achievement motivation.

## Achievement Motivation and Gender

Abrol (1977) found that boys have higher achievement motivation than girls.

Kalpana, Mallela (2003) reported no significant difference between the parental encouragements given to Bi.P.C. and M.P.C. students, boys and girls.

O'Malley and Johnston (2001) reported that male students drink more than female students.

Naik (1979) found no sex difference, no difference between achievement motivation and achievement scores.

Sharma Brajesh Kumar, Subramanian and Narayana (2006) showed no relationship between self-concept and achievement motivation among boys while a significant positive relationship between self-concept and achievement motivation among girls.

Tripathi, R.C. (1986) noticed that achievement motivation of boys and girls was highly correlated with intelligence and achievement.

## Achievement Motivation and Intelligence

Chauhan, S.S. (1984) found that the achievement motivation of students differed significantly at different levels of intelligence, viz., high, middle and low.

Jain, S. (1983) found that the high intelligent high achievement motivation group was significantly better in concept formation ability by employing patristic strategy.

Rajpoot (1984) found no interaction effect between intelligence and achievement motivation.

## Achievement Motivation and Personality

Siddiqui (1979) observed that personality has a positive correlation with achievement motivation.

Singh (1984) found that self-concept was significantly and positively related to achievement motivation.

Gupta (1979) reported a positive relationship between psychological test and achievement motivation.

Pandiya (1979) did not found any relationship between religious outlook and achievement motivation.

**Achievement Motivation and Socio-economic Status**

Rajpoot (1984) found no interaction effect between socio-economic status and achievement motivation.

**Drinking**

Bronnam, et.al. (1987) identified eight studies examining different motives for alcohol consumption among college students. Two general types of drinking motives typically emerge in students of college studies are drinking for social purposes and drinking for emotional escape or relief.

Johnston L.D., O'Malley, P.M., Bachman, J.G. (2001) reported that many students entering college bring established drinking practices with them. Thirty percent of 12th graders report binge drinking in high school, slightly more report having 'been drunk', and almost three-quarters report drinking in the past years.

Johnston L.D., O'Malley, P.M., Bachman, J.G. (2001) observed that the prevalence of periodic heavy or high-risk drinking is greatest among young adults aged 19 to 24; and among young adults, college students have the highest prevalence of high-risk drinking.

Schulenberg, J. Maggs, J.L., Long, S.W., Sher, K.J., Gotham, H.J., Baer, J.S., Kivlahan, D.R., Marlatt, G.A., and Zucker, R.A. (2001) reported that the heavy drinking rates of college students surpass those of their non-college peers, and this rapid increase in heavy drinking over a relatively short period of time can contribute to difficulties with alcohol and with the college transition in general.

Baer (2002) reported that drinking among college students is often associated with impulsivity/sensation seeking or the regulation of negative emotional states including depression and anxiety.

Spear (2002) observed that the adolescents may show reduced sensitivity to alcohol effects and increased sensitivity to stressors, both of which may influence drinking behaviour.

**Drinking and Locality**

Weschsler, H., Davenport, A., Dowdall, G., Moeykens, B. and Castillo, S. (1994) reported that colleges located more than a mile from the nearest alcohol outlet had lower rates of heavy episodic drinking than colleges with outlets within a mile.

**Drinking and Gender**

Weschsler, H., Davenport, A., Dowdall, G., Moeykens, B. and Castillo, S. (1994) reported significant differences with black men and especially black women reporting significantly lower rates of heavy episodic drinking than their peers.

Dowdall, GW, Crawford, M and Wechsler, H. (1998) reported important differences in drinking behaviour between those women who attend women's colleges and those women who attend coeducational colleges.

**Drinking and Personality**

Astin (1993) reported that college drinking research needs to link with a more complex organizational understanding of higher education, including how going to college influences student behaviour.

Toomey and Wagenaar (2002) observed the importance of the social environment in individual drinking behaviour, but suggest that the social environment is substantially shaped by public and institutional policies.

Perkins (2002) observed negative consequences like fatal and non-fatal injuries, hangover and vomiting, alcohol poisoning, blackouts, unintended sexual activity, sexually transmitted diseases, etc., that result from alcohol consumption of college students. These consequences impact the individuals who drink, their fellow students and the institutions they attend.

Perkins (2002) reported that campus norms for alcohol use, perceived or real, are a strong predictors of individual student drinking.

Presley, Meilman and Leichliter (2002) reported the relationship of collegiate environments to student drinking. He emphasized the importance of a cogent model of student drinking that incorporates the environment, student campus culture and individual factors.

## Achievement Motivation and Academic Achievement

Singhaulakh, S.P. (1979) reported that motivation was found to have a significant relationship with better performance and achievement.

As the above cited studies are not equivalent to the proposed study, hence this study on achievement motivation and academic achievement of alcoholic and non-alcoholic college students.

# Design of the Study

> "Whatever you think, that you will be. If you think yourselves weak, weak you will be; if you think yourselves strong, strong you will be".
>
> —*Swami Vivekananda*

## Method of Research

Research is a systematic enquiry seeking facts through objective verifiable methods in order to discover the relationship among them and to deduce from them the broad principles or laws. Therefore, the very success of a research work depends upon collecting the necessary information. Several methods of collecting information are developed to assist the research. Every survey expert has his own ideas of selecting the best method of collecting information. But, it cannot be uniform to all. Selection of the method depends on the type of information to be gathered and the sources of information to be consulted. For the present study, the normative survey method was chosen.

Survey means viewing and interpreting things rigorously and comprehensively. Now-a-days, survey method is a popular way of collecting data and analyzing the results statistically and systematically. This method is suitable to this study as this one is a status study.

## OPERATIONAL DEFINITIONS OF KEY TERMS

The operational definitions of the important key terms used in the present study on "A Study of Achievement Motivation and Academic Achievement of Alcoholic and Non-Alcoholic College Students" are defined herewith:

### 1. Study

Study refers to a systematic investigation which is objective and research-oriented.

### 2. Alcoholism

- The medical condition caused by drinking too much alcohol regularly. — Oxford Advanced Learners Dictionary
- Physiological addiction to alcohol usually accompanied by psychological dependence. — Mastering Psychology, Lefton and Valvante
- Alcoholism is a chronic, progressive, and often fatal disease. It is a primary disorder and not a symptom of other diseases or emotional problems.

### 3. Alcoholic Student

Alcoholic student is a person who regularly drinks too much alcohol and cannot easily stop drinking, so that it has become illness.

### 4. Non-Alcoholic Student

A student person who does not take or consume alcohol regularly.

### 5. Achievement Motivation

Achievement motivation refers to the desire of a person to meet the standards of excellence.

### 6. Academic Achievement

Academic achievement can be understood as one's learning attainments, accomplishments or proficiencies in performing a given task in education.

### 7. College Students

Students studying in the arts, science, commerce, engineering, medical, computer, and management colleges.

## VARIABLES OF THE STUDY

Variables are the conditions or characteristics that the experimenter manipulates, controls or observes. There are mainly three types of variables, namely, independent, dependent and intervening. The independent variables are those variables which do not change on manipulation by the experimenter. The dependent variables are those variables which change on manipulations made by the experimenter. The intervening variables are those variables which are dependent both on dependent and independent variables.

For the present study, the following independent variables were chosen:

1. *Arts students:* MA alcoholic and MA non-alcoholic students.
2. *Medical students:* MBBS alcoholic and MBBS non-alcoholic students.
3. *Engineering students:* BTech alcoholic and BTech non-alcoholic students.
4. *Computer students:* MCA alcoholic and MCA non-alcoholic students.
5. *Management students:* MBA alcoholic and MBA non-alcoholic students.

Since no previous studies were conducted on the variables, namely, arts, engineering, medical, computers and management students who are alcoholic and non-alcoholic, this study was considered.

## HYPOTHESES OF THE STUDY

Hypothesis is a tentative generalization, which provides basis to the whole study to be tested by facts. It is a shrewd and intelligent guess, supposition, inference, hunch, provisional statement, tentative generalization to the existence of some fact, condition or relationship relative to some phenomena which serves to explain already known facts in a given area of knowledge and which guides the search for new truth on the basis of empirical evidence.

The hypothesis to be tested in this study is "null hypothesis." Ordinarily, a null hypothesis is a statement to believe that there is no relation to the independent and dependent variable. Once it is formulated, depending on the outcome, it will be either accepted or rejected.

For the present study, the following hypotheses were framed:

*Hypothesis 1:* There is no high academic achievement in alcoholic and non-alcoholic college students.

*Hypothesis 1A:* There is no significant difference in the academic achievement of alcoholic and non-alcoholic arts students.

*Hypothesis 1B:* There is no significant difference in the academic achievement of alcoholic and non-alcoholic medical students.

*Hypothesis 1C:* There is no significant difference in the academic achievement of alcoholic and non-alcoholic engineering students.

*Hypothesis 1D:* There is no significant difference in the academic achievement of alcoholic and non-alcoholic computer students.

*Hypothesis 1E:* There is no significant difference in the academic achievement of alcoholic and non-alcoholic management students.

*Hypothesis 2:* There is no high achievement motivation in alcoholic and non-alcoholic college students.

*Hypothesis 2A:* There is no significant difference in the achievement motivation of alcoholic and non-alcoholic arts students.

*Hypothesis 2B:* There is no significant difference in the achievement motivation of alcoholic and non-alcoholic medical students.

*Hypothesis 2C:* There is no significant difference in the achievement motivation of alcoholic and non-alcoholic engineering students.

*Hypothesis 2D:* There is no significant difference in the achievement motivation of alcoholic and non-alcoholic computer students.

*Hypothesis 2E:* There is no significant difference in the achievement motivation of alcoholic and non-alcoholic management students.

*Hypothesis 3:* There is no significant difference in the academic achievement of alcoholic and non-alcoholic college students.

*Hypothesis 4:* There is no significant difference in the achievement motivation of alcoholic and non-alcoholic college students.

*Hypothesis 5:* There is no correlation between academic achievement and achievement motivation of alcoholic and non-alcoholic college students.

*Hypothesis 5A:* There is no correlation between academic achievement and achievement motivation of alcoholic and non-alcoholic arts students.

*Hypothesis 5B:* There is no correlation between academic achievement and achievement motivation of alcoholic and non-alcoholic medical students.

*Hypothesis 5C:* There is no correlation between academic achievement and achievement motivation of alcoholic and non-alcoholic engineering students.

*Hypothesis 5D:* There is no correlation between academic achievement and achievement motivation of alcoholic and non-alcoholic computer students.

*Hypothesis 5E:* There is no correlation between academic achievement and achievement motivation of alcoholic and non-alcoholic management students.

## SAMPLE OF THE STUDY

A sample is a smaller representation of the larger whole. A sample contains primarily sampling units and a slice of the population representing the universe. A sample must possess the following essential characteristics to provide accurate results. They are representativeness, adequacy, and homogeneity, lack of bias, smallness in size, accuracy and completeness.

As the sample is a slice of the population, the population for the study refers to all the college-going students studying MA, MBBS, BTech., MCA and MBA courses in the Colleges located in Guntur district.

Sampling is the easiest method of social investigation. The purpose of sampling is to draw inferences concerning the universe. There are three elements in the process of sampling. They are selection of the sample, collection of information and drawing inferences. According to Cornell, "sampling is the process by which a relatively small number of individuals are selected or analyzed in order to find out something about the entire population or the universe from which it is selected".

In any research, various methods are utilized for selection of samples. After a detailed study of all the methods, the stratified random sampling method was selected for the present study.

Stratified random sampling method is followed as this method of sample selection assures each individual element in the universe an equal chance of being chosen. This is suitable for the present study as the universe considered for the study is homogenous, the college students.

In order to reduce the sampling error, a sample of 500 was chosen. In this study, the strata divided are represented in the following table:

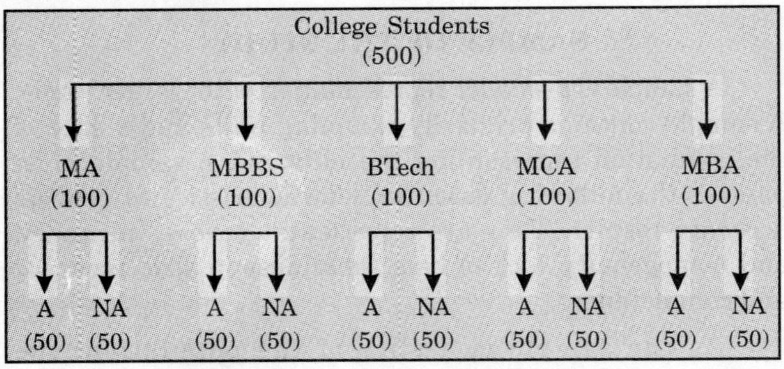


A – Alcoholic college students

NA – Non-alcoholic college students

As all the sample colleges (Guntur Medical College, Guntur; N.R.I. Medical College, Kakani, Guntur Dt.; Katuri Medical College, Chinakondrupadu, Guntur Dt.; R.V.R. & J.C. College of Engineering, Chowdavaram, Guntur Dt.; V.V. Institute of Technology, Guntur; Loyola Institute of Technology and Management, Sattenapalli, Guntur Dt.; J.K.C. College, Guntur; Vignan College, Palakaluru, Guntur Dt.; Hindu College, Guntur; T.J.P.S. College, Guntur; S.G.M.R. P.G. College, Guntur; Mahatma Gandhi College, Guntur; A.C. College, Guntur; Acharya Nagarjuna University, Nagarjuna Nagar, Guntur Dt.) are having more than 3000 students each and the Guntur city is housing most of these students; several of these students are addicted to alcohol. The alcoholics were identified by interacting with peers first and later with staff of these colleges.

## TOOLS OF THE STUDY

A research tool is used for the purpose of data collection and is a tool which has reliability and validity. Reliability is the degree of consistency that the instrument or procedure demonstrates. Validity is that quality of a data gathering instrument or procedure that enables it to measure what it is supposed to measure.

A research tool plays a major role in any worthwhile research, as it is the sole factor in determining sound data and in arriving at perfect conclusions about the problem or study in hand, which ultimately helps in providing suitable remedial measures to the problem concerned. The selection and use of a tool can be done in two ways. The first one is to construct a tool independently by the researcher and the second one is to select a standardized tool that is already available in the field of study.

### Measurement of Achievement Motivation

The tool used in the present study to measure the achievement motivation is 'Achievement Motivation Scale' standardized by Beena Shah. The Achievement Motivation Scale of Beena Shah consists four factors, namely:

1. Need for academic success;
2. Need for vocational achievement;
3. Need for social achievement; and
4. Need for skill achievement.

The Achievement Motivation Scale (AMS) is a three point scale. Each statement is followed by three alterative responses. The alternatives are arranged in order of one's inclination towards achievement in the areas of academic success, vocational achievement, social achievement and achievement skills. 1, 2 and 3 marks are awarded respectively for alternatives (a), (b) and (c) statements. Thus, the scale value lies between 40 and 120.

## Measurement of Academic Achievement

The annual examination scores of the sample were collected from the respective colleges and were converted into percentages. Each sampling unit score lies between 0 and 100. These scores were used as raw scores for statistical calculations and to accept or reject the formulated hypotheses.

## Administration of the Tool and Data Collection

The AMS was administered personally on the college going alcoholic and non-alcoholic students studying in different colleges and the sample was asked to respond to the statements. Before giving the tool to the sampling units, the researcher explained the purpose of the present investigation. Directions given on the cover sheet were read out to the sample and specific instructions were given. Then the sample answered the scale leisurely.

After the AMS was administered, the annual previous exam marks of those sampling units were collected from the heads of the institutions.

# Analysis of Data

> "Student safety is of paramount importance; we simply have to make certain that our [alcohol prevention] programme is working".
>
> —*William Jenkins*

Analysis of the data is the most skilled task of all stages of research. It depends on the judgement and skill of the researcher. It should be done by the researcher and should not be entrusted to another person. Analysis of data means studying the tabulated material in order to determine inherent facts or meanings. It involves breaking down complex factors into simple ones and putting the parts in new arrangements for the purpose of interpretation.

The first step in the analysis of data is a critical examination of the assembled data. This includes the researcher to think and analyze the data in the next method of analysis, coding. Coding involves assigning symbols to each response, the purpose of which is to translate raw data into symbols. This depends on proper coding of responses. Coding can be done by the respondent or observer or the interviewer. There may be difficulties in coding due to inadequacy of data, inefficiency of the coder and lack of editing or scrutinizing of the available data. Editing can be helpful for coding and for improving the quality of data collection.

Tabulation is a means of recording classification in a compact form in such a way so as to facilitate comparisons. Data is arranged in rows and columns to facilitate mathematical and statistical operations. It is of great help in the analysis and interpretation of data. While tabulating the data, the purpose of the study has to be kept in mind.

The method of analysis chosen for a particular study depends upon the nature of objectives formulated, hypotheses to be tested, and usefulness of the study. Statistical methods are the mathematical techniques used to facilitate the interpretation of numerical data secured from groups of individuals or group of observations or a single individual. A basic knowledge about statistics becomes inevitable for research workers for systematic analysis and accurate and precise interpretation of data.

For the present study titled "A Study of Achievement Motivation and Academic Achievement of Alcoholic and Non-Alcoholic College Students", several statistical techniques were used to perform the analysis. After collecting the data from five hundred college students, the analysis was performed keeping in view the objectives framed, hypotheses formulated, type of data collected, type of tools used, etc.

The highest academic achievement score or the lowest academic achievement score one can get is 100 or 0 respectively. The academic achievement is classified as per government public examination procedure: Low: 0-49 marks (fail or third class), Average: 50-59 marks (second class) and High: 60-100 marks (first class or distinction).

The highest achievement motivation score or the lowest achievement motivation score one can get is 120 or 40 respectively. The achievement motivation is classified as per AMS values: Low: 40-65, Average: 66-95, and High: 96-120 scores.

The correlation is identified as: Complete positive correlation: +1, Very high positive correlation: +0.90 to +0.99, High positive correlation: +0.70 to +0.90, Middle/ Average correlation: +0.40 to +0.70, Low positive correlation: +0.20 to +0.40, Very low positive correlation: Less than 0.20, Zero correlation: 0.00, Very low negative correlation: Less than -0.20, Low negative correlation: -0.20 to -0.40, Middle/ Average correlation: -0.40 to -0.70, High negative correlation: -0.70 to -0.90, Very high negative correlation: -0.90 to -0.99, Complete negative correlation: -1.00.

The mean, standard deviation, critical ratio, correlation, etc., were employed for making analysis of raw data.

### Hypothesis 1

*"There is no high academic achievement in alcoholic and non-alcoholic college students"*.

To test the validity of hypothesis 1, the mean of the academic achievement scores was calculated.

**Table 4.1: Academic Achievement of College Students**

| Sample | Size | Mean | Standard Deviation |
|---|---|---|---|
| Whole | 500 | 60.46 | 8.23 |

From the mean value of Table 4.1, it is evident that there was an average level of academic achievement in college students.

The hypothesis that "there is no high academic achievement in alcoholic and non-alcoholic college students" can be accepted as the college students possess high level of academic achievement.

### Hypothesis 1A

*"There is no significant difference in the academic achievement of alcoholic and non-alcoholic arts students"*.

To test the validity of hypothesis 1A, the following calculations were carried out:

**Table 4.2: Comparison of Academic Achievement of Alcoholic and Non-alcoholic Arts Students**

| Variable | Sample Size | Mean | S.D. | Mean Difference | Standard Error of Means | Critical Ratio |
|---|---|---|---|---|---|---|
| Alcoholic | 50 | 52.52 | 6.978 | 13.44 | 1.4 | 9.6* |
| Non-alcoholic | 50 | 65.96 | 7.059 | | | |

* Significant at 0.05 level.

From the values of Table 4.2, it is evident that the academic achievement level in alcoholic and non-alcoholic arts college students was significantly different. The alcoholic arts students possess an average level of academic achievement compared to non-alcoholic arts students who possess a high level of academic achievement.

The hypothesis that "there is no significant difference in the academic achievement of alcoholic and non-alcoholic arts students" can be rejected as there is a significant difference in the level of academic achievement of alcoholic and non-alcoholic arts students.

## Hypothesis 1B

*"There is no significant difference in the academic achievement of alcoholic and non-alcoholic medical students".*

To test the validity of hypothesis 1B, the following calculations were made.

From the values of Table 4.3, it is clear that the academic achievement level in alcoholic and non-alcoholic medical college students was significantly different since the alcoholic medical students possess an average level of academic achievement compared to non-alcoholic medical students who possess a high level of academic achievement.

**Table 4.3: Comparison of Academic Achievement of Alcoholic and Non-alcoholic Medical Students**

| Variable | Sample Size | Mean | S.D. | Mean Difference | Standard Error of Means | Critical Ratio |
|---|---|---|---|---|---|---|
| Alcoholic | 50 | 55.38 | 4.655 | 13.08 | 1.064 | 12.29* |
| Non-alcoholic | 50 | 68.46 | 5.922 | | | |

* Significant at 0.05 level.

The hypothesis that "there is no significant difference in the academic achievement of alcoholic and non-alcoholic medical students" can be rejected as there is a significant difference in the level of academic achievement of alcoholic and non-alcoholic medical students.

### Hypothesis 1C

"*There is no significant difference in the academic achievement of alcoholic and non-alcoholic engineering students*".

To test the validity of hypothesis 1C, the following calculations were carried out.

**Table 4.4: Comparison of Academic Achievement of Alcoholic and Non-alcoholic Engineering Students**

| Variable | Sample Size | Mean | S.D. | Mean Difference | Standard Error of Means | Critical Ratio |
|---|---|---|---|---|---|---|
| Alcoholic | 50 | 55.1 | 3.87 | 11.62 | 0.987 | 11.77* |
| Non-alcoholic | 50 | 66.72 | 5.814 | | | |

* Significant at 0.05 level.

From the values of Table 4.4, it is evident that the academic achievement level in alcoholic and non-alcoholic engineering college students was significantly different since the alcoholic engineering students possess an average level of academic achievement compared to non-alcoholic engineering students who possess a high average level of academic achievement.

The hypothesis that "there is no significant difference in the academic achievement of alcoholic and non-alcoholic engineering students" can be rejected as there is a significant difference in the level of academic achievement of alcoholic and non-alcoholic engineering students.

## Hypothesis 1D

*"There is no significant difference in the academic achievement of alcoholic and non-alcoholic computer students"*.

To test the validity of hypothesis 1D, the following calculations were made:

**Table 4.5: Comparison of Academic Achievement of Alcoholic and Non-alcoholic Computer Students**

| Variable | Sample Size | Mean | S.D. | Mean Difference | Standard Error of Means | Critical Ratio |
|---|---|---|---|---|---|---|
| Alcoholic | 50 | 54.3 | 5.146 | 11.8 | 0.936 | 12.60* |
| Non-alcoholic | 50 | 66.18 | 4.17 | | | |

* Significant at 0.05 level.

From the values of Table 4.5, it is clear that the academic achievement level in alcoholic and non-alcoholic computer college students was significantly different since the alcoholic computer students possess an average level of academic achievement compared to non-alcoholic computer students who possess a high level of academic achievement.

The hypothesis that "there is no significant difference in the academic achievement of alcoholic and non-alcoholic computer students" can be rejected as there is a significant difference in the level of academic achievement of alcoholic and non-alcoholic computer students.

## Hypothesis 1E

*"There is no significant difference in the academic achievement of alcoholic and non-alcoholic management students"*.

To test the validity of hypothesis 1E, the following calculations were calculated:

**Table 4.6: Comparison of Academic Achievement of Alcoholic and Non-alcoholic Management Students**

| Variable | Sample Size | Mean | S.D. | Mean Difference | Standard Error of Means | Critical Ratio |
|---|---|---|---|---|---|---|
| Alcoholic | 50 | 54.50 | 3.68 | 11.5 | 1.038 | 11.07* |
| Non-alcoholic | 50 | 66.00 | 6.2 | | | |

* Significant at 0.05 level

From the values of Table 4.6, it is evident that the academic achievement level in alcoholic and non-alcoholic management college students was significantly different since the alcoholic management students possess an average level of academic achievement compared to non-alcoholic management students who possess a high level of academic achievement.

The hypothesis that "there is no significant difference in the academic achievement of alcoholic and non-alcoholic management students" can be rejected as there is a significant difference in the level of academic achievement of alcoholic and non-alcoholic management students.

## Hypothesis 2

"There is no high achievement motivation in alcoholic and non-alcoholic college students."

To test the validity of hypothesis 2, the mean of the achievement motivation scores was calculated.

**Table 4.7: Achievement Motivation of College Students**

| Sample | Size | Mean | Standard Deviation |
|---|---|---|---|
| Whole | 500 | 69.08 | 15.30 |

From the mean value of Table 4.7, it is evident that there was an average level of achievement motivation in college students.

The hypothesis that "there is no high achievement motivation in alcoholic and non-alcoholic college students" can be rejected as the college students possess an average level of achievement motivation.

**Hypothesis 2A**

"*There is no significant difference in the achievement motivation of alcoholic and non-alcoholic arts students*".

To test the validity of hypothesis 2A, the following calculations were carried out:

**Table 4.8: Comparison of Achievement Motivation of Alcoholic and Non-alcoholic Arts Students**

| Variable | Sample Size | Mean | S.D. | Mean Difference | Standard Error of Means | Critical Ratio |
|---|---|---|---|---|---|---|
| Alcoholic | 50 | 50.80 | 11.50 | 27.56 | 2.432 | 11.33* |
| Non-alcoholic | 50 | 78.36 | 12.79 | | | |

* Significant at 0.05 level.

From the values of Table 4.8, it is evident that the achievement motivation level in alcoholic and non-alcoholic arts college students was significantly different since the alcoholic arts students possess a low level of achievement motivation compared to non-alcoholic arts students who possess an average level of achievement motivation.

The hypothesis that "there is no significant difference in the achievement motivation of alcoholic and non-alcoholic arts students" can be rejected as there is a significant difference in the level of achievement motivation of alcoholic and non-alcoholic arts students.

**Hypothesis 2B**

*"There is no significant difference in the achievement motivation of alcoholic and non-alcoholic medical students."*

To test the validity of hypothesis 2B, the following calculations were carried out:

**Table 4.9: Comparison of Achievement Motivation of Alcoholic and Non-alcoholic Medical Students**

| Variable | Sample Size | Mean | S.D. | Mean Difference | Standard Error of Means | Critical Ratio |
|---|---|---|---|---|---|---|
| Alcoholic | 50 | 63.30 | 7.86 | 20.50 | 1.69 | 12.13* |
| Non-alcoholic | 50 | 83.80 | 9.09 | | | |

* Significant at 0.05 level.

From the values of Table 4.9, it is evident that the achievement motivation level in alcoholic and non-alcoholic medical college students was significantly different since the alcoholic medical students possess a low level of achievement motivation compared to non-alcoholic medical students who possess an average level of achievement motivation.

The hypothesis that "there is no significant difference in the achievement motivation of alcoholic and non-alcoholic medical students" can be rejected as there is a significant difference in the level of achievement motivation of alcoholic and non-alcoholic medical students.

**Hypothesis 2C**

*"There is no significant difference in the achievement motivation of alcoholic and non-alcoholic engineering students."*

To test the validity of hypothesis 2C, the following calculations were carried out:

**Table 4.10: Comparison of Achievement Motivation of Alcoholic and Non-alcoholic Engineering Students**

| Variable | Sample Size | Mean | S.D. | Mean Difference | Standard Error of Means | Critical Ratio |
|---|---|---|---|---|---|---|
| Alcoholic | 50 | 62.10 | 7.30 | 17.0 | 1.91 | 8.9* |
| Non-alcoholic | 50 | 79.10 | 11.40 | | | |

* Significant at 0.05 level.

From the values of Table 4.10, it is evident that the achievement motivation level in alcoholic and non-alcoholic engineering college students was significantly different since the alcoholic engineering students possess an a low level of achievement motivation compared to non-alcoholic engineering students who possess an average level of achievement motivation.

The hypothesis that "there is no significant difference in the achievement motivation of alcoholic and non-alcoholic engineering students" can be rejected as there is a significant difference in the level of achievement motivation of alcoholic and non-alcoholic engineering students.

**Hypothesis 2D**

"*There is no significant difference in the achievement motivation of alcoholic and non-alcoholic computer students*".

To test the validity of hypothesis 2D, the following calculations were carried out:

From the values of Table 4.11, it is evident that the achievement motivation level in alcoholic and non-alcoholic computer college students was significantly different since the alcoholic computer students possess a low level of achievement motivation compared to non-alcoholic computer students who possess an average level of achievement motivation.

**Table 4.11: Comparison of Achievement Motivation of Alcoholic and Non-alcoholic Computer Students**

| Variable | Sample Size | Mean | S.D. | Mean Difference | Standard Error of Means | Critical Ratio |
|---|---|---|---|---|---|---|
| Alcoholic | 50 | 53.0 | 8.7 | 26.2 | 2.038 | 12.90* |
| Non-alcoholic | 50 | 79.2 | 11.5 | | | |

* Significant at 0.05 level.

The hypothesis that "there is no significant difference in the achievement motivation of alcoholic and non-alcoholic computer students" can be rejected as there is a significant difference in the level of achievement motivation of alcoholic and non-alcoholic computer students.

## Hypothesis 2E

*"There is no significant difference in the achievement motivation of alcoholic and non-alcoholic management students."*

To test the validity of hypothesis 2E, the following calculations were carried out:

**Table 4.12: Comparison of Achievement Motivation of Alcoholic and Non-alcoholic Management Students**

| Variable | Sample Size | Mean | S.D. | Mean Difference | Standard Error of Means | Critical Ratio |
|---|---|---|---|---|---|---|
| Alcoholic | 50 | 60.40 | 8.43 | 20.44 | 1.58 | 12.93* |
| Non-alcoholic | 50 | 80.84 | 7.36 | | | |

* Significant at 0.05 level.

From the values of Table 4.12, it is evident that the achievement motivation level in alcoholic and non-alcoholic management college students was significantly different since the alcoholic management students possess a low level of achievement motivation compared to non-alcoholic arts students who possess an average level of achievement motivation.

The hypothesis that "there is no significant difference in the achievement motivation of alcoholic and non-alcoholic management students" can be rejected as there is a significant difference in the level of achievement motivation of alcoholic and non-alcoholic management students.

## Hypothesis 3

"*There is no significant difference in the academic achievement of alcoholic and non-alcoholic college students.*"

To test the validity of hypothesis 3, the following calculations were carried out:

**Table 4.13: Comparison of Academic Achievement of Alcoholic and Non-alcoholic College Students**

| Variable | Sample Size | Mean | S.D. | Mean Difference | Standard Error of Means | Critical Ratio |
|---|---|---|---|---|---|---|
| Alcoholic | 250 | 54.36 | 4.88 | 1.208 | 0.49 | 2.46* |
| Non-alcoholic | 250 | 66.57 | 6.09 | | | |

* Significant at 0.05 level.

From the values of Table 4.13, it is evident that the academic achievement level in alcoholic and non-alcoholic arts college students was significantly different since the alcoholic college students possess an average level of academic achievement compared to non-alcoholic college students who possess a high level of academic achievement.

The hypothesis that "there is no significant difference in the academic achievement of alcoholic and non-alcoholic college students" can be rejected as there is a significant difference in the level of academic achievement of alcoholic and non-alcoholic college students.

## Hypothesis 4

*"There is no significant difference in the achievement motivation of alcoholic and non-alcoholic college students."*

To test the validity of hypothesis 4, the following calculations were carried out:

**Table 4.14: Comparison of Achievement Motivation of Alcoholic and Non-alcoholic College Students**

| Variable | Sample Size | Mean | S.D. | Mean Difference | Standard Error of Means | Critical Ratio |
|---|---|---|---|---|---|---|
| Alcoholic | 50 | 57.90 | 10.19 | 22.36 | 0.93 | 13.54* |
| Non-alcoholic | 50 | 80.26 | 10.70 | | | |

* Significant at 0.05 level.

From the values of Table 4.14, it is evident that the achievement motivation level in alcoholic and non-alcoholic college students was significantly different since the alcoholic college students possess a low level of achievement motivation compared to non-alcoholic college students who possess an average level of achievement motivation.

The hypothesis that "there is no significant difference in the achievement motivation of alcoholic and non-alcoholic college students" can be rejected as there is a significant difference in the level of achievement motivation of alcoholic and non-alcoholic college students.

## Hypothesis 5

*"There is no correlation between academic achievement and achievement motivation of alcoholic and non-alcoholic college students."*

To test the validity of hypothesis 5, the correlation between academic achievement and achievement motivation was calculated.

**Table 4.15: Correlation between Academic Achievement and Achievement Motivation of Alcoholic and Non-alcoholic College Students**

| Variable | Sample Size | Mean | S.D | Correlation |
|---|---|---|---|---|
| Academic Achievement | 500 | 60.46 | 8.23 | 0.57 |
| Achievement Motivation | 500 | 69.08 | 15.30 | |

From the correlation value of Table 4.15, it is evident that there exists an average or middle level positive correlation between academic achievement and achievement motivation of alcoholic and non-alcoholic college students.

The hypothesis that "there is no correlation between academic achievement and achievement motivation of alcoholic and non-alcoholic college students" can be rejected as there is average/middle level positive correlation between academic achievement and achievement motivation of alcoholic and non-alcoholic college students.

## Hypothesis 5A

"*There is no correlation between academic achievement and achievement motivation of alcoholic and non-alcoholic arts students.*"

To test the validity of hypothesis 5A, the following calculations were carried out:

From the correlation values of Table 4.16, it is evident that there exists a very low negative correlation between academic achievement and achievement motivation of alcoholic arts students and a very low positive correlation between academic achievement and achievement motivation of non-alcoholic arts students.

**Table 4.16: Correlation between Academic Achievement and Achievement Motivation of Alcoholic and Non-alcoholic Arts Students**

| | Variable | Sample Size | Mean | S.D | Correlation |
|---|---|---|---|---|---|
| Alcoholics | Academic Achievement | 50 | 52.52 | 6.97 | -0.14 |
| | Achievement Motivation | 50 | 50.80 | 11.50 | |
| Non-alcoholics | Academic Achievement | 50 | 65.96 | 7.059 | 0.03 |
| | Achievement Motivation | 50 | 78.36 | 12.79 | |

The hypothesis that "there is no correlation between academic achievement and achievement motivation of alcoholic and non-alcoholic arts students" can be rejected as there is a negative and positive correlation respectively between academic achievement and achievement motivation of alcoholic and non-alcoholic arts students.

### Hypothesis 5B

"*There is no correlation between academic achievement and achievement motivation of alcoholic and non-alcoholic medical students*".

To test the validity of hypothesis 5B, the following calculations were carried out:

From the correlation values of Table 4.17, it is evident that there exists a low positive correlation between academic achievement and achievement motivation of alcoholic medical students and a very low negative correlation between academic achievement and achievement motivation of non-alcoholic medical students.

**Table 4.17: Correlation between Academic Achievement and Achievement Motivation of Alcoholic and Non-alcoholic Medical Students**

| Variable | | Sample Size | Mean | S.D | Correlation |
|---|---|---|---|---|---|
| Alcoholics | Academic Achievement | 50 | 55.38 | 4.655 | 0.25 |
| | Achievement Motivation | 50 | 63.30 | 7.860 | |
| Non-alcoholics | Academic Achievement | 50 | 68.46 | 5.922 | -0.004 |
| | Achievement Motivation | 50 | 83.80 | 9.090 | |

The hypothesis that "there is no correlation between academic achievement and achievement motivation of alcoholic and non-alcoholic medical students" can be rejected as there is a low positive and very low negative correlation between academic achievement and achievement motivation of alcoholic and non-alcoholic medical students.

### Hypothesis 5C

"*There is no correlation between academic achievement and achievement motivation of alcoholic and non-alcoholic engineering students*".

To test the validity of hypothesis 5C, the following calculations were carried out:

From the correlation values of Table 4.18, it is evident that there exists a very low positive correlation between academic achievement and achievement motivation of alcoholic engineering students and also a very low negative correlation between academic achievement and achievement motivation of non-alcoholic engineering students.

**Table 4.18: Correlation between Academic Achievement and Achievement Motivation of Alcoholic and Non-alcoholic Engineering Students**

| Variable | | Sample Size | Mean | S.D | Correlation |
|---|---|---|---|---|---|
| Alcoholics | Academic Achievement | 50 | 55.10 | 3.87 | 0.17 |
| | Achievement Motivation | 50 | 62.10 | 7.30 | |
| Non-alcoholics | Academic Achievement | 50 | 66.72 | 5.814 | 0.06 |
| | Achievement Motivation | 50 | 79.10 | 11.40 | |

The hypothesis that "there is no correlation between academic achievement and achievement motivation of alcoholic and non-alcoholic medical students" can be rejected as there is a very low correlation between academic achievement and achievement motivation of alcoholic and non-alcoholic engineering students.

## Hypothesis 5D

"*There is no correlation between academic achievement and achievement motivation of alcoholic and non-alcoholic computer students*".

To test the validity of hypothesis 5D, the following calculations were carried out:

From the correlation values of Table 4.19, it is evident that there exists a very low positive correlation between academic achievement and achievement motivation of alcoholic and non-alcoholic computer students.

The hypothesis that "there is no correlation between academic achievement and achievement motivation of alcoholic and non-alcoholic computer students" can be rejected as there is a very low positive correlation between academic achievement and achievement motivation of alcoholic and non-alcoholic computer students.

**Table 4.19: Correlation between Academic Achievement and Achievement Motivation of Alcoholic and Non-alcoholic Computer Students**

| Variable | | Sample Size | Mean | S.D | Correlation |
|---|---|---|---|---|---|
| Alcoholics | Academic Achievement | 50 | 54.30 | 4.17 | 0.09 |
| | Achievement Motivation | 50 | 53.00 | 8.70 | |
| Non-alcoholics | Academic Achievement | 50 | 62.10 | 5.146 | 0.04 |
| | Achievement Motivation | 50 | 79.20 | 11.50 | |

## Hypothesis 5E

*"There is no correlation between academic achievement and achievement motivation of alcoholic and non-alcoholic management students."*

To test the validity of hypothesis 5E, the following calculations were carried out:

From the correlation values of Table 4.20, it is evident that there exists a low positive correlation between academic achievement and achievement motivation of alcoholic management students and a low negative correlation between academic achievement and achievement motivation of non-alcoholic medical students.

The hypothesis that "there is no correlation between academic achievement and achievement motivation of alcoholic and non-alcoholic medical students" can be rejected as there is a low positive and low negative correlation between academic achievement and achievement motivation of alcoholic and non-alcoholic management students respectively.

**Table 4.20: Correlation between Academic Achievement and Achievement Motivation of Alcoholic and Non-alcoholic Management Students**

| Variable | | Sample Size | Mean | S.D | Correlation |
|---|---|---|---|---|---|
| Alcoholics | Academic Achievement | 50 | 54.50 | 3.68 | 0.3 |
| | Achievement Motivation | 50 | 60.40 | 8.43 | |
| Non-alcoholics | Academic Achievement | 50 | 66.00 | 6.20 | -0.24 |
| | Achievement Motivation | 50 | 80.84 | 7.36 | |

# Summary, Conclusions Discussion and Suggestions

"We dare not let alcohol blemish your bright promise".

—*Thomas K. Hearn*

## Summary

Motivation is the driving force behind all the actions of an individual. It is based on emotions and achievement-related goals. There are different forms of motivation including extrinsic, intrinsic, physiological, and achievement motivation. Achievement motivation is the need for success or the attainment of excellence. Individuals will satisfy their needs through different means, and are driven to succeed for varying reasons, both internal and external.

Motivation is a generic term referring to a family of concepts used to explain initiation, direction, maintenance and termination of activities undertaken by living organisms. It impels or pushes the organisms into activity, giving them direction. It is useful to explain the variability observed in behaviour. In particular, the choice of behaviour is the main question because living beings are always active. The fluctuation or change in preference for activity or choice of goal leads to choosing one activity over the other. In general, people approach certain goals or engage in activities that are expected to have desirable outcomes and avoid activities that lead to unpleasant or aversive outcomes. However, many people do like challenges, undertake difficult tasks and seek pleasure in engaging in adventures. These persons have different kinds and levels of motivation.

Achievement motivation refers to the desire of a person to meet standards of excellence. The need to achieve, also known as n-Arch, energises directs the behaviour and influences the perception of situations. It is not biological but shows a tremendous effect on human behaviour. People differ in the degree to which they experience this need.

Achievement motivation is the desire to excel at tasks. This means that individuals with high achievement motivation tend to set goals that are neither too easy nor extremely difficult. Easy tasks do not present a challenge and are of no interest. Extremely difficult goals increase the risk of failure.

Early studies conducted by McClelland (1961) and other researchers around the globe on achievement motivation are correlated with high scholastic performance and success in business. Such people opt for moderately difficult tasks. They are future-oriented and persist more on the task. Also they are upwardly mobile. McClelland found that, in general, protestant countries, where independence and achievement are valued, were economically more advanced. The parents train children to be self supportive and develop greater autonomy. Some researchers have found that females experience a fear of success, since striving for success may reduce feminity in the eyes of others.

Academic achievement, as excellence in all academic disciplines, in class as well as extra-curricular activities. It includes excellence in sporting, behaviour, confidence, communication skills, punctuality, assertiveness, arts, culture, and the like. Academic achievement or performance refers to how students deal with their studies and how they cope with or accomplish different tasks given to them by their teachers. Academic performance is the ability to study and remember facts and being able to communicate your knowledge verbally or down on paper.

The academic achievement can be understood as one's learning attainments, accomplishments or proficiencies in performing a given task. Achievement is directly related to the growth and development of pupils in educational situations, where teaching and learning go hand-in-hand. The concept of achievement involves the interaction of three factors, viz., aptitude for learning, readiness for learning and opportunity for learning. The concept also involves health and physical fitness, motives and desires and emotional balances of the individuals in the fulfillment of the given tasks. Achievement in education implies one's knowledge, understanding and skills in a specified subject or a group of subjects.

Drinking behaviour is a complex one, and there is a need to broaden the range of issues studied, particularly extending analysis to the economic, political and ecological factors that have thus far received far less study than the psycho-social issues. Alcoholism is a chronic, progressive and often fatal disease. It is a primary disorder and not a symptom of other diseases or emotional problems. The alcohol consumption can be categorized into moderate drinking, hazardous (heavy) drinking and harmful drinking. The chemistry of alcohol allows it to affect nearly every type of cell in the body, including those in the central nervous system. After prolonged exposure to alcohol, the brain adapts to the changes that alcohol makes and becomes dependent on it. The severity of the disease is influenced by factors such as genetics, psychology, culture and response to physical pain.

Identifying the very importance of achievement motivation and academic achievement in academic courses of professional and arts students, this study has been undertaken to study the levels of achievement motivation and academic achievement of and their relationship in alcoholic and non-alcoholic college students.

The present study was confined to Guntur district. The sample was drawn from the college students studying in the Colleges of arts, medical, engineering, computers and management. The sample size chosen for the present study was 500 college alcoholic and non-alcoholic students.

The objectives of the study were:

- To find out the academic achievement of alcoholic and non-alcoholic college students.
- To find out the academic achievement of alcoholic and non-alcoholic arts students.
- To find out the academic achievement of alcoholic and non-alcoholic medical students.
- To find out the academic achievement of alcoholic and non-alcoholic engineering students.
- To find out the academic achievement of alcoholic and non-alcoholic computer students.
- To find out the academic achievement of alcoholic and non-alcoholic management students.
- To find out the achievement motivation of alcoholic and non-alcoholic college students.
- To find out the achievement motivation of alcoholic and non-alcoholic arts students.
- To find out the achievement motivation of alcoholic and non-alcoholic medical students.
- To find out the achievement motivation of alcoholic and non-alcoholic engineering students.
- To find out the achievement motivation of alcoholic and non-alcoholic computer students.
- To find out the achievement motivation of alcoholic and non-alcoholic management students.

- To find out the significant difference in the academic achievement of alcoholic and non-alcoholic college students.
- To find out the difference in the achievement motivation of alcoholic and non-alcoholic college students.
- To find out the correlation between academic achievement and achievement motivation of alcoholic and non-alcoholic college students.
- To find out the correlation between academic achievement and achievement motivation of alcoholic and non-alcoholic arts students.
- To find out the correlation between academic achievement and achievement motivation of alcoholic and non-alcoholic medical students.
- To find out the correlation between academic achievement and achievement motivation of alcoholic and non-alcoholic engineering students.
- To find out the correlation between academic achievement and achievement motivation of alcoholic and non-alcoholic computer students.
- To find out the correlation between academic achievement and achievement motivation of alcoholic and non-alcoholic management students.

The normative survey method was used in the present study. This method investigates into the conditions and relationships that exist at present in the context of academic achievement and achievement motivation.

Variable is a condition or characteristic which the experimenter manipulates, controls or observes. For the present study, the variables chosen were:

- Arts students (MA alcoholic and MA non-alcoholic college students).
- Medical students (MBBS alcoholic and MBBS non-alcoholic college going students).

- Engineering students (BTech alcoholic and BTech non-alcoholic college students).
- Computer students (MCA alcoholic and MCA non-alcoholic college students).
- Management students (MBA alcoholic and MBA non-alcoholic college students).

Hypotheses are the guesses or tentative generalizations which provide a basis to the whole study to be tested by facts. For the present study, the hypotheses framed were:

- There is no high academic achievement in alcoholic and non-alcoholic college students.
  - There is no significant difference in the academic achievement of alcoholic and non-alcoholic arts students.
  - There is no significant difference in the academic achievement of alcoholic and non-alcoholic medical students.
  - There is no significant difference in the academic achievement of alcoholic and non-alcoholic engineering students.
  - There is no significant difference in the academic achievement of alcoholic and non-alcoholic computer students.
  - There is no significant difference in the academic achievement of alcoholic and non-alcoholic management students.
- There is no high achievement motivation of alcoholic and non-alcoholic college students.
  - There is no significant difference in the achievement motivation of alcoholic and non-alcoholic arts students.
  - There is no significant difference in the achievement motivation of alcoholic and non-alcoholic medical students.

- There is no significant difference in the achievement motivation of alcoholic and non-alcoholic engineering students.
- There is no significant difference in the achievement motivation of alcoholic and non-alcoholic computer students.
- There is no significant difference in the achievement motivation of alcoholic and non-alcoholic management students.

➢ There is no significant difference in the academic achievement of alcoholic and non-alcoholic college students.

➢ There is no significant difference in the achievement motivation of alcoholic and non-alcoholic college students.

➢ There is no correlation between academic achievement and achievement motivation of alcoholic and non-alcoholic college students.

- There is no correlation between academic achievement and achievement motivation of alcoholic and non-alcoholic arts students.
- There is a no correlation between academic achievement and achievement motivation of alcoholic, non-alcoholic medical students.
- There is no correlation between academic achievement and achievement motivation of alcoholic and non-alcoholic engineering students.
- There is no correlation between academic achievement and achievement motivation of alcoholic and non-alcoholic computer students.
- There is no correlation between academic achievement and achievement motivation of alcoholic and non-alcoholic management students.

A sample is a small group which represents all the traits and characteristics of the population. The alcoholic and non-alcoholic students studying in colleges of arts, medical, engineering, computers and management of Guntur district were selected as population. The stratified random sampling technique was used in selecting the sample. The sample size was 500 (five hundred) college students, consisting 100 students each from MA, MBBS, BTech, MCA and MBA courses.

A research tool is a tool used for the purpose of data collection. The tools used in the present study were the previous year's academic percentages of the students and the Achievement Motivation Scale of Beena Shah.

For the analysis of the data, statistical techniques, viz., mean, standard deviation, critical ratio and correlation were used.

## CONCLUSIONS AND DISCUSSION

From the analysis of data, the following conclusions are drawn and are followed by necessary discussion and suggestions:

1. **The alcoholic and non-alcoholic college students are holding high academic achievement.**

The present state of academic achievement may be due to the nature of course work as the college professional course students encounter totally new content as well as new practical experiences in learning. This may also be due to the awareness that the mastery of subject helps in getting a proper professional job, for which the college students need to learn and work more when compared to their previous education.

The college students may enhance their academic achievement by developing better study habits, by participating in all seminars intensively, by participating in yoga and meditation and by developing more achievement motivation. Their academic achievement can also be improved by mingling with co-students in performing different kinds of academic activities like quiz competitions, debates, etc., as per the norms and standards laid down in the course work.

2. **The alcoholic arts students are possessing an average level of academic achievement. The non-alcoholic arts students are possessing a high level of academic achievement. There is a significant difference in the academic achievement of alcoholic and non-alcoholic arts students.**

The common course material provided, the common goals and aspirations of becoming a good employee, the undifferentiated aim of getting a better job, the mental as well as physical maturity, the surrounding environment, their attitudes, etc., might have played a legitimate role in having a significant difference in the level of academic achievement of alcoholic and non-alcoholic arts students.

Both the alcoholic and non-alcoholic arts students can enhance their academic achievement by developing better learning skills. To make students love learning and to use the art of learning to apply themselves in their academic subjects, developing a positive attitude towards college and quality education is a dire need.

The alcoholics should stay away from alcohol as it is effecting their academic achievement.

3. **The alcoholic medical students are possessing an average level of academic achievement. The non-alcoholic medical students are possessing a high level of academic achievement. There is a significant difference in the academic achievement of alcoholic and non-alcoholic medical students.**

Though the alcoholic and non-alcoholic medical students strive hard equally for better academic achievement in their studies, the alcoholism is putting the alcoholics away from expectations. So, the student's level of initiative, enthusiasm and ability to self start in all curricular components should be encouraged. Personal attitudes and interests towards a course also play a very important role, so they must be encouraged in positive direction.

The importance of high academic achievement or the desire to be a good doctor should be emphasized. A student should choose a career by choice rather than do a job on the wish of others. Self discipline and responsibility should be inculcated in the students to enhance their academic achievement.

The alcoholics need to think again and again before taking alcohol as it has been a cause for low achievement.

4. **The alcoholic engineering students are possessing an average level of academic achievement. The non-alcoholic engineering students are holding a high level of academic achievement. There is a significant difference in the academic achievement of alcoholic and non-alcoholic engineering students.**

Methods of time management and self discipline in academic pursuits should become the prior responsibility of the students. Strategies for learning from lengthy and complex reading assignments should be effectively planned, implemented and evaluated.

Analytical and critical thinking skills that are essential to excel in their academics should be developed. Stress management and life style choices that foster academic success must be inculcated in one's college life.

The alcoholics should think of the bad affects of alcoholism and keep themselves away from it.

5. **The alcoholic computer students are possessing an average level of academic achievement. The non-alcoholic computer students are holding a high level of academic achievement. There is a significant difference in the academic achievement of alcoholic and non-alcoholic computer students.**

The expansion of information technologies makes computers accessible practically to all students at college as well as at home. Computers can be used to help with homework or for free time activities. Looking for information online involves the solution of educable resources in order to extract, organize and integrate information which develops problem solving skills in the college course subjects. Students should focus on the conditions necessary for effective learning while using computers.

The alcoholics should understand the ill affects of alcoholism and do not consume it.

6. **The alcoholic management students are having an average level of academic achievement. The non-alcoholic management students are with a high level of academic achievement. There is a significant difference in the academic achievement of alcoholic and non-alcoholic management students.**

The teaching learning material used is to be in accordance with the recent needs of the students and in accordance with the recent technological developments. The quality of instruction need to be increased.

Students can enhance personally their academic achievement by better perception and has being well adjusted in their college life with the changing circumstances of the day-to-day. They must be prepared physically, mentally and socially as strong individuals so as to be role models to their co-students and colleagues.

The alcoholic as well as non-alcoholic college students should increase their levels of academic achievement as it is one of the parameters in the selection process of jobs and in career development.

The alcoholic management students need to think about the sufferings that arise out of alcoholism and stay away from it to help themselves and also others.

7. **The alcoholic and non-alcoholic college students are holding an average level of achievement motivation.**

The present status of achievement motivation may be due to the students' perceptions of college experiences, which play a significant role achievement motivation. Student satisfaction at every time is necessary for a continued motivation. This may be due to the profession they select in which they have to be role models to the community members and the society.

The alcoholic and non-alcoholic college students can enhance their achievement motivation by understanding of the old students' learning proactivities which may be valuable in helping them, developing a greater understanding of their unique goals and needs in an educational system that was originally established to facilitate growth, training and education of young adults.

8. **The alcoholic arts students are possessing a low level of achievement motivation. The non-alcoholic arts students are holding an average level of achievement motivation. There is a significant difference in the achievement motivation of alcoholic and non-alcoholic arts students.**

The arts subjects help the students develop literary (language) skills such as listening, speaking, reading and writing along with creative arts. The arts encourage divergent thinking and problem solving skills, enabling students to think creatively.

Access to and participation in the arts helps decrease and prevent negative behaviour in the youth.

As the alcoholism is a hindrance to creativity, they should stay away from it.

9. **The alcoholic medical students are possessing a low level of achievement motivation. The non-alcoholic medical students are holding an average level of achievement motivation. There is a significant difference in the achievement motivation of alcoholic and non-alcoholic medical students.**

The behaviour of an individual can differ due to the motivational drives of that an individual is introduced to environmental and cultural factors in the college life. These factors will strongly influence an individual's behaviour despite his own intrinsic motives for success.

As future doctors, the medical students must stay away from alcohol consumption as it hampers their achievement due to low achievement motivation.

10. **The alcoholic engineering students are possessing a low level of achievement motivation and the non-alcoholic engineering students are holding an average level of achievement motivation. There is a significant difference in the achievement motivation of alcoholic and non-alcoholic engineering students.**

College environment goals will mainly direct the actions of staff, students and others to the extent that they adopt the knowledge of human functioning and the actions consistent with such knowledge. By exercising certain behaviours that facilitate learning, they directly control situational factors in which learning occurs.

The alcoholic engineering students should understand the risks associated with alcoholism and engineering profession, and avoid alcohol consumption and develop achievement motivation.

11. **The alcoholic computer students are possessing a low level of achievement motivation compared to non-alcoholics who are possessing an average level of achievement motivation. There is a significant difference in the achievement motivation of alcoholic and non-alcoholic computer students.**

Seeking ways to demonstrate how motivation plays an important role in ones educational settings, one can encourage instructional programmes that offer alternatives with the idea that they might be more effective in motivating students. By using extrinsic reward systems judiciously and inviting motivational speakers to the college, one can enhance their achievement motivation.

The alcoholic students should not become pray to alcoholism and develop better achievement motivation to enhance their academic achievement.

12. **The alcoholic management students are possessing a low level of achievement motivation. The non-alcoholic management students are with an average level of achievement motivation. There is a significant difference in the achievement motivation of alcoholic and non-alcoholic management students.**

Achievement motivation can be enhanced by bringing in outstanding speakers to the college meetings, placing names of high achieving students on the honor roll, publishing an annual report of academic achievement and mailing it to parents, and displaying academic awards and trophies in the college.

The alcoholics need to compare their achievement with non-alcoholics and enhance their achievement motivation as it is one of the guiding factors of academic achievement.

13. **The alcoholic college students are possessing an average level of academic achievement and the non-alcoholic college students are with high academic achievement. There is a significant difference in the academic achievement of alcoholic and non-alcoholic college students.**

Making academic achievement as a frequent topic of discussion among students, teachers and other staff, it can be shown that success is important to the student. By recognizing the variety of ways through which a student can succeed can also improve the academic achievement of college students.

As there is a significant difference in the academic achievement of alcoholic and non-alcoholic students, the alcoholic students should discard the habit of drinking and try to improve their level of academic achievement. The college, in general, and the family, in particular, and the community at large need to try to help the alcoholic students become non-alcoholics and settle well in their lives and careers.

14. **The alcoholic college students are possessing a low level of achievement motivation. The non-alcoholic college students are possessing an average level of achievement motivation. There is a significant difference in the achievement motivation of alcoholic and non-alcoholic college students.**

Motivation can be characterized by a student's personal interest in a given task. The magnitude of motivation is influenced by the psychological environment of a college, that is, by the meaning given to the overall educational experiences.

As a college community, demonstrate to students how motivation plays an important role in one's life, both professionally and personally, and ensure that restructuring the programmes will address the issues related to student motivation.

Inclusion of alcoholics and non-alcoholics in every academic activity will promote their achievement motivation.

15. **There is average/middle level positive correlation between academic achievement and achievement motivation of alcoholic and non-alcoholic college students.**

The academic circles need to support and implement programmes that help avoid alcoholism in college students and help them do well in academic achievement and achievement motivation as they are interrelated.

16. **There is a very low negative correlation between academic achievement and achievement motivation of alcoholic arts students and there is a very low positive correlation between academic achievement and achievement motivation of non-alcoholic arts students.**

Well designed and executed arts education leads to overall improved academic performance and also achievement motivation. It builds skills necessary for workplace success and develops a positive influence on the lives of the students.

17. **There is a low positive correlation between academic achievement and achievement motivation of alcoholic medical students, and there is a very low negative correlation between academic achievement and achievement motivation of non-alcoholic medical students.**

Development of intrinsic motivation in students is an important goal for educators because of its inherent importance for future motivation as well as for students' effective learning. High motivation and engagement in learning have consistently been linked to increased levels of student success.

**18. There is a very low positive correlation between academic achievement and achievement motivation of alcoholic and non-alcoholic engineering students.**

By helping the students experience the moments of self-actualization and self-realization, students can discover for themselves the pleasure of acquiring new knowledge. This helps the students acquire self-motivation leading to a perceptual desire to learn and to achieve better.

**19. There is a very low positive correlation between academic achievement and achievement motivation of alcoholic and non-alcoholic computer students.**

An extremely important component of the climate of the effective college is the presence of visible symbols which illustrate and confirm what is considered to be important in the college. The strength of one's motivation to act depends on the importance attached to the goal in question and ones judgement about its achievability; motivational strength also depends on ones judgement about how successful a particular behaviour will be in moving towards goal achievement.

**20. There is a low positive correlation between academic achievement and achievement motivation of alcoholic management students, and there is a low negative correlation between academic achievement and achievement motivation of non-alcoholic management students.**

Practices that ensure clarity and completeness of assignments and appropriate review procedures for different types of case studies must be effectively evaluated. Demonstrating thinking skills such as long term planning, critiquing and focused attention can reap positive social and academic benefits. Thus, the link between academic achievement and achievement motivation be established and enhanced.

The college teachers, and the social and educational environment should make the college students feel comfortable during their course period. The college students should enhance their academic achievement and achievement motivation by adopting better strategies. Better skills, good relations with peers and teachers, good teaching learning material, effective audio-visual aids, quality instruction, self motivation, adjustment, yoga and meditation, better study habits, good life skills, appropriate aspirations, etc., will help the college students in enhancing their academic achievement and achievement motivation. The college students should develop and improve all of the above in order to master the skills and knowledge and to become expert professionals in future after rolling out of the colleges.

Teachers must build a community of learning that cares most about helping students achieve more in academics through an atmosphere of cooperation and understanding. Teacher teams should develop curriculum and work together with local artists to present and enhance new learning experiences. Teachers should learn that the creation of independent student learning activities allow students to develop their own learning skills in a different way from teacher led classroom instruction and encourage students to take risk in order to increase their understanding.

## SUGGESTIONS FOR FUTHER RESEARCH

The present study, A Study on Achievement Motivation and Academic Achievement of Alcoholic and Non-Alcoholic College Students, brings to light a good number of new areas to be studied by future researchers. The areas and variables that are not covered by this study may be put to test to enlighten the other associated factors. So, the researchers may think of the following areas of study in detail.

1. Studies may be taken up to study the impact of alcoholism on students and their academic achievement.

2. Studies may be taken up to identify the various factors which make a student to become alcoholic and the measures to eradicate alcoholism in educational campuses.
3. Studies may be taken up on experimental basis to inculcate, nourish and promote achievement motivation and academic achievement in alcoholics.
4. Studies may be taken up to identify the impact of various factors on alcoholics and their behaviour and studies.
5. Studies may be taken up to identify the background reasons of former alcoholic students and their settlement of life and their present position in society.
6. Studies may be conducted on the physical, psychological, personal, sociological and economical problems of alcoholic students.
7. Studies may be conducted on family background, and feelings and experiences of alcoholic students.
8. Studies may be taken up to suggest suitable measures to stop excessive drinking and bringe drinking in college.
9. Studies may be conducted how to enhance the academic achievement and achievement motivation in alcoholic college students.
10. Studies may be taken up on suitable therapies and withdrawal symptoms to get rid of the problem of consuming alcohol in college students.
11. Studies can be taken up to know the effect of factors like age, stage of education, socio-economic status, attitude, adjustment, creativity and other factors on academic achievement and achievement motivation
12. Studies can be taken up to know the influence of academic achievement and achievement motivation on the overall personality of the student.

13. Studies can be considered to know the impact of education, employment, economic status, etc., of parents on the academic achievement and achievement motivation of children/students.
14. Studies can be undertaken to find out the influence of school environment, home environment, teachers and co-students on the academic achievement and achievement motivation of students.

# Bibliography


Abraham, P.A. (1969). *An Experimental Study of Certain Personality Traits and Achievement of Secondary School Pupils.* Ph.D. Psychology, Kerala University.

Acharya, P. (1991). *Personality Correlates of Matching Figure Test: An Emperical Study.* M.Phil. Psychology, Utkal University.

Aggarwal, Y.P. (1998) *Statistical Methods.* New Delhi: Sterling Publishing House

Ahuja, Malvinder and Tachanut, Yaiuva (2006). *Effectiveness of Multimedia CAI and Conventional Learning Conditions in Relation to Persistence of Professional College Students.* University News, 44, (52), 13-21.

Alegaokar, P.M. (1981). *Effect of Physical Achievement on Intelligence.* Ph.D. Education, Poona University.

Aruna, N.S. (1981). *A Study of the Factors Influencing the Achievement of Standard VII Students Belonging to SC and ST's Whose Medium of Instruction is Kannada.* Ph.D. Education, Mysore University.

Baer (2002). *Student Factors: Understanding Individual Variation in College Drinking.* Journal of Studies on Alcohol. Supplement No. 14, March 2002.

Baruah, Mukul Kumar (1988). *Socio-psychological Characteristics of Professional and Non-professional Students*. Ph.D. Education, Dibrugarh University.

Best, John W. and James, V. Khan (2005). *Research in Education,* 9th Edition. New Delhi: Prentice Hall of India Private Limited.

Bhattacharya, Anjana (1989). *A Cross-sectional Study of some Differential Aptitudes of Secondary School Students*. Ph.D. Education, Kalyani University.

Bhargava, K. (1980). *Self-disclosure as Related to Academic Competence and Personality (with special reference to Neurotic and Schizophrenic Personalities*). Ph.D. Psychology, Agra University.

Bhaskara Rao, D., Vijaya, K. and Sridevi, C. (1995). *Achievement in Social Studies*. New Delhi: Discovery Publishing House.

Bronnam, et.al. (1987). *College Drinking, What It Is, and What To Do About It: A Review of the State of the Science*. Journal of Studies on Alcohol. Supplement No. 14, March 2002.

Buch, M.B., Chief Editor (1978-1983). *Third Survey of Research in Education*. Baroda: CASE, M.S. University of Baroda.

Buch, M.B., Chief Editor (1983-1988). *Fourth Survey of Research in Education*. New Delhi: NCERT.

Buch, M.B., Chief Editor (1988-1992). *Fifth Survey of Research in Education*. New Delhi: NCERT.

Burwani, Rupa G. (1991). *An Enquiry into the Nature of Self-concept in the Area of Competence and Its Impact on Mental Health and Academic Achievement*. Ph.D. Education, Visva Bharati University.

Chatterji, P.S. (1983). *A Comparative Study of Personality, Intelligence and Achievement Motivation of Students in Different Academic Groups*. Ph.D. Education, Patna University.

Chaudhary, N. (1971). *The Relationship Between Achievement Motivation and Anxiety, Intelligence, Sex, Social Class and Vocational Aspiration*. Ph.D. Psychology, Punjab University.

Chauhan, S.S. (1984). *A Comparative Study of the Achievement Motivation of ST and SC's of Himachal Pradesh in Relation to Their Intelligence, Socio-Economic Status*. Ph.D. Education, Himachal Pradesh University.

Clapp, J.D. and McDonnell, A.L. (2000). *College Drinking, What It Is, and What To Do About It: A Review of the State of the Science*. Journal of Studies on Alcohol. Supplement No. 14, March 2002.

DeJong (2002). *The Role of Mass Media Campaigns in Reducing High Risk Drinking Among College Students*. Journal of Studies on Alcohol. Supplement No. 14, March 2002.

Dennis Thombs (1991). *A Test of the Perceived Norms Model to Explain Drinking Patterns Among University Athletes*. Journal of Studies on Alcohol. Supplement No. 14, March 2002.

Dhall, Taruna C. and Salni, Madhu (2008). *Academic Performance of Elementary School Children of Working and Non-Working Mothers*. EduTracks, 7, (5), 41-43.

Dowdall, GW, Crawford, M and Wechsler, H. (1998). *Binge Drinking Among American College Women: A Comparison of Single-sex and Co-educational Institutions*. Psychol. Women Q. 22: 705-715.

Dubois, Alverson Stanley (1979). *Educational Psychology and Institutional Decisions*. Illinois: The Dorsey Press Homewood.

Dutt, N.K. (2003). *Psychological Foundations of Education*. New Delhi: Doaba House.

Edger, Marlow and Bhaskara Rao, D. (2004). *Teaching Social Studies Successfully*. New Delhi: Discovery Publishing House.

Garga, Satish Chandra (1951). *Memory Span in Children of 12+*. Unpublished Dissertation (M.Ed.), Allahabad University.

Gnanaguru, Selvaraj A. and Kumar, Suresh M. (2008). *Under-achievement of B.Ed. Students in Relation to their Home Environment and Attitude Towards Teaching*. EduTracks, 7, (12), 20-22.

Goode, William, J. and Paul K. Hatt (1983). *Methods in Social Research*. New Delhi: McGraw-Hill.

Gowri, Prasad P. (2005). *A Study of Stress on Secondary School Teacher's in Guntur District*. M.Ed. Dissertation, Acharya Nagarjuna University.

Grewal, P.S. *Methods of Statistical Analysis*. New Delhi: Sterling Publishing House.

Gupta, Alka (1992). *A Study of Students Academic Satisfaction as related to their Personality Needs and Personal Values*. Ph.D. Education, Allahabad University.

Gupta, B.D. (1988). *Intelligence, Adjustment and Personality Needs of Effective Teachers in Science and Arts*. Ph.D. Education, Agra University.

Hingston, R.W. and Howland, J. (2002). *Comprehensive Community Interventions to Promote Health: Implications for College Age Drinking Problems*. Journal of Studies on Alcohol Supplement 14: 226-240.

Jain, S. (1983). *Concept Formation as a Function of Verbal Intelligence and Achievement Motivation*. Ph.D Education, Rajasthan University.

Jantli, R.T. (1988). *Relationship Between Teacher Behaviour, Pupil Personality and Pupil Growth Outcome*. Ph.D. Education, Karnataka University.

Jogi, J.K. (1984). *The Effect of response on Achievement at Different Levels: With reference to Intelligence and Taxonomic Categories through a Programme in Micro Economics*. Ph.D. Education, Himachal Pradesh University.

Johnston, L.D. O'Malley, P.M., Bachman, J.G. (2001). *Monitoring the Future National Survey Results on Drug Use, 1975-2000. Volume I: Secondary School Students*. NIH Publication No. 01-4924. Bethesda, MD: National Institute on Drug Abuse.

Johnston LD, O'Malley P.M., Bachman, J.G. (2001). *Monitoring the Future National Survey Results on Drug Use, 1975-2000. Volume II:* College Students and Adult Ages 19-40. NIH Publication No. 01-4925. Bethesda, MD: National Institute on Drug Abuse.

Jordan Sorenson (1990). *College Drinking, What It Is, and What To Do about It: A Review of the State of the Science*. Journal of Studies on Alcohol. Supplement No. 14, March 2002.

Joshi, Renuka (1989). *A Study of Creativity in Relation to Personality, Locus of Control and Alienation*. Ph.D. Psychology, Punjab University.

Kabu, C.L. (1980). *A Psychological Analysis of the Mathematically Gifted at the Secondary and Higher Levels of Education*. Ph.D. Education, Jammu University.

Kalpana, Mallela (2003). *A Study of the Parental Encouragement on the Academic Career of Intermediate Students*. M.Ed. Dissertation, Acharya Nagarjuna University.

Kochar, S.K. (1979). *Teaching of Social Studies*. New Delhi: Sterling Publishers Pvt. Ltd.

Konwar, L.N. (1989). *A Study of Socialisation Practices at Home and School and Development of Personal*

*Achievement Motivation among Secondary School Pupils in Assam.* Ph.D. Education, Dibrugarh University.

Koteswara, M.N. and Ramachandra Reddy, B. (2001). *Impact of 14 Personality Factors on Reading Achievement of High School Students.* The Educational Review, 44, (10), 4-7.

Kumari, Darshana (1986). *Intellectual Commitment and Educational Interest in relation to certain Cognitive and Non-Cognitive Variables.* Ph.D. Education, Jammu University.

Kumari, Indira (1990). *A Study of Development of Logical Thinking in Pre-Adolescents.* Ph.D. Education, Maharshi Dayanand University.

Kumari, Indira and Dagaur, B.S. (1992). *Piagetian Concepts of Conservation, Seriation and Classification in Relation to Intelligence.* Indian Educational Review, 27, (4), 73-85.

Kundu, C.L. (1989). *Personality Development.* New Delhi: Sterling Publishers Pvt. Limited.

Kuppuswamy, B. (2003). *Advanced Educational Psychology.* New Delhi: Sterling Publishers Private Limited.

Lall, R. and Schankler, S.L. (1990). *College Drinking, What It Is, and What To Do About It: A Review of the State of the Science.* Journal of Studies on Alcohol. Supplement No. 14, March 2002.

Liebert, Obert M. and John, M. Neale (1977). *Psychology.* USA: John Wiley and Sons, Inc.

Lohithaksh (2003). *Dictionary of Education — A Practical Approach.* New Delhi: Kanishka Publishing and Distributors.

Mangal, S.K. (1987). *Abnormal Psychology.* New Delhi: Sterling Publishers Private Limited.

Molstad, S., Mc Millan, C., Kher, N. and Kilcoyne, M. (1998). *College Drinking, What It Is, and What To Do About It: A Review of the State of the Science.* Journal of Studies on Alcohol. Supplement No. 14, March 2002.

Naik, Ramesh H. (2006). *Effect of Teachers Personality, Attitude and Teaching Effectiveness Rating on Students Academic Achievement.* Experiments in Education, 34, (4), 4-10.

Nanda, S.K. (2003). *Methodology of Educational Research and Educational Statistics.* New Delhi: Doaba Private House.

Natarajan, R. and Balan, K. (2003). *Performance of Arts Based Teachers and Science Based Teachers of Primary Schools.* The Educational Review, 46, (2), 18-19.

Nibedita, Das (2004). *Fundamentals of Teaching.* New Delhi: Dominant Publishing and Distributors.

O'Malley and Johnston (2001). *Epidemiology of Alcohol and Other Drug Use Among American College Students.* Journal of Studies on Alcohol. Supplement No. 14, March 2002.

Pal, Anita (1988). *A Study of Competition and Co-operation in High School Children as Related to Personality and Parental Education.* Ph.D. Psychology, Punjab University.

Paramesh, C.R. (1972). *Creativity and Personality.* First Edition, Janatha Book House, Madras-600014, India.

Pareek, D.L. (1990). *A Comparative Study of the Self-Concept, Personality Traits and Aspirations of the Adolescents studying in Central Schools, State.*

Pathak, A.N. (1989). *Creativity and Personality.* New Delhi: Amar Prakashan Publishers.

Patil, I. (1982). *A Psychological Study of Intellectually Superiors.* Ph.D. Psychology, Karnataka University.

Perkins (2002). *Surveying the Damage: A Review of Research on Consequences of Alcohol Misuse in College Populations.* Journal of Studies on Alcohol. Supplement No. 14, March 2002.

Perkins (2002). *Social Norms and the Prevention of Alcohol Misuses in Collegiate Contexts.* Journal of Studies on Alcohol. Supplement No. 14, March 2002.

Presley, Meilman and Leichliter (2002). *College Factors That Influence Drinking. College Drinking, What It Is, and What To Do About It: A Review of the State of the Science.* Journal of Studies on Alcohol. Supplement No. 14, March 2002.

Rakesh Lall (1991). *College Drinking, What It Is, and What To Do About It: A Review of the State of the Science. Journal of Studies on Alcohol.* Supplement No. 14, March 2002.

Ramiah, L. (1990). *A Relational Study of Parent Involvement and Self-concept of Standard IX Students in Devakottai Educational District.* M.Phil. Education, Alagappa University.

Rao, D.G. (1965). *A Study of Some Factors Related to Scholastic Achievement.* Ph.D. Education, Delhi University.

Rao, N.C.S. (1951). *Strategy in Concept Learning.* Allahabad Indian International Publications, 95-96.

Ray, Mrinmarji (1988). *Ethnic Difference in Intelligence.* Indian Educational Review, 23, (2), 114-119.

Reddy, Y. Sudhakara and D. Bhaskara Rao (2003). *Creativity in Adolescents.* New Delhi: Discovery Publishing House.

Rummel, Frances J. (1958). *An Introduction to Research Procedure in Education.* New York: Harper and Brothers.

Saulade, S.D. (1989). *Verbal Maze Learning: It's Cognitive and Personality Determinants.* Ph.D. Psychology, Nagpur University.

Saxena, P.C. (1981). *A Study of Interests, Need Patterns and Adjustment Problems of Over and Under Achievement.* Model Institute of Education and Research, Jammu.

Schaller, M., Kemeny, A. and Maltzman, I. (1992). *College Drinking, What It Is, and What To Do About It: A Review of the State of the Science.* Journal of Studies on Alcohol. Supplement No. 14, March 2002.

Schulenberg J, Maggs JL, Long SW, Sher KJ, Gotham HJ, Baer JS, Kivlahan DR, Marlatt GA, and Zucker RA (2001). *The Problem of College Drinking: Insights from a Developmental Perspective.* Alcoholism: Clinical and Experimental Research 25 (3): 473-477.

Sharma, Brajesh Kumar, Subramanian K.B. and Narayana U.L. (2006). *Relationship Between Self-concept, Academic Motivation and Achievement in Mathematics: A Gender Comparison.* EduTracks, 5, (9), 29-32.

Sharma, N.K. (1981). *A Comparative Study of Extroversion, Neuroticism, Achievement Motivation and Adjustment of Tribal, Rural and Urban Youth of Himachal Pradesh.* Ph.D. Psychology, Panjab University.

Shah, Suhasini H. (1992). *A Study of the Effectiveness of Educational Programmes for Developing Skills of Thinking.* Ph.D. Education, Saurashtra University.

Sharma, K. (1981). *Some Socio-economic Characteristics and Intellectual Abilities of High School Students.* Ph.D. Psychology, Mag. University.

Sharma, K.L. (1978). *A Comparative Study of Self-concept of High and Low Achievement of Intelligence Group of Students of Class Tenth in Urban Schools of Bareilly.* Ph.D. Education, Agra University.

Spear (2002). *The Adolescent Brain and the College Drinker: Bioligical Basis of Propensity to Use and Misuse Alcohol.* Journal of Studies on Alcohol. Supplement No. 14, March 2002.

Sidhu, K.S. (1984). *Methodology of Research in Education.* New Delhi: Sterling Publishing House.

Singhaulakh, S.P. (1979). *Student Motivation to Work.* Ph.D. Education, Rajasthan University.

Sunil Kiran, K.S. (2005). *A Study of the Impact of Emotional Intelligence on Academic Achievement of Junior College Students.* M.Ed. Dissertation, Acharya Nagarjuna University.

Tiwari, Govind and Roma, Pal (1984). *Abnormal Psychology— Dynamic Approach.* Agra: Vinod Pustak Mandir.

Toomey and Wagenaar (2002) *Environmental Policies to Reduce College Drinking: Options and Research Findings.* Journal of Studies on Alcohol. Supplement No. 14, March 2002.

Tripathi, R.C. (1986). *Motivation and Its Correlates of High School Students of East Uttar Pradesh.* Ph.D. Education, Gorakhpur University.

Venkata, Rao B. (2004). *A Comparative Study of the Personality Characteristics of High and Low Academic Achievers.* M.Ed. Dissertation, Acharya Nagarjuna University.

Vidhu, M. (1968). *The Relationship Between Neuroticism and Extroversion to Intelligence and Educational Achievement at Different Age Levels.* Ph.D. Psychology, Punjab University.

Weschsler, H., Davenport, A., Dowdall, G., Moeykens, B. and Castillo, S. (1994). *Health and Behavioural Consequences of Bringe Drinking in College: A National Survey of Students at 140 Campuses.* JAMA 272: 1672-1677.

Weschsler, H, Kuo M and Dowdall GW (2000). *Environmental Correlates of Underage Alcohol Use and Related Problems of College Students.* American Journal of Preventive Medicine 19(1): 24-29.

Yadav, R.S. (1991). *Factors Affecting Intelligence.* Indian Educational Review, 26, (1), 95-106.

**Additional Reading**

Bhaskara Rao, Digumarti (1994). *Scientific Aptitude.* New Delhi: Ashish Publishing House. ISBN 81-7024-658-X.

Bhaskara Rao, Digumarti (1995). *Animal Kingdom.* New Delhi: Discovery Publishing House. ISBN 81-7141-274-2.

Bhaskara Rao, Digumarti (1995). *Batracology.* New Delhi: Discovery Publishing House. ISBN 81-7141-279-3.

Bhaskara Rao, Digumarti (1997). *Scientific Attitude.* New Delhi: Discovery Publishing House. ISBN 81-7141-381-1.

Bhaskara Rao, Digumarti (1996). *Scientific Attitude vis-à-vis Scientific Aptitude.* New Delhi: Discovery Publishing House. ISBN 81-7141-308-0.

Bhaskara Rao, Digumarti (2004). *Scientific Attitude, Scientific Aptitude and Achievement.* New Delhi: Discovery Publishing House. ISBN 81-7141-781-7.

Bhaskara Rao, Digumarti (2004). *Educational Administration.* New Delhi: Discovery Publishing House. ISBN 81-7141-842-2.

Bhaskara Rao, Digumarti (2004). *Issues in School Education.* New Delhi: Discovery Publishing House. ISBN 81-8356-025-3.

Bhaskara Rao, Digumarti, Editor (1996). *Encyclopaedia of Education For All,* 5 Volumes. New Delhi: APH Publishing Corporation. ISBN 81-7024-759-4 (set).

*Vol. I* Education For All: The World Conference. *ISBN 81-7024-760-8.*

*Vol. II* Education For All: The EPA-9 Summit. *ISBN 81-7024-761-6.*

*Vol. II* Education For All: Quality Education For All. *ISBN 81-7024-762-6.*

*Vol. IV* Education For All: Planning and Monitoring. *ISBN 81-7024-763-4.*

*Vol. V* *Education For All: The Indian Scenario.* ISBN 81-7024-764-0.

Bhaskara Rao, Digumarti, Editor (1999). *International Encyclopaedia of AIDS*, 11 Volumes. New Delhi: Discovery Publishing House. ISBN 81-7141-522-6 (set).

*Vol. 1* Introduction to HIV/AIDS. *ISBN 81-7141-523-7.*

*Vol. 2* HIV/AIDS — Issues and Challenges, *2 Parts. ISBN 81-7141-524-5.*

*Vol. 3* HIV/AIDS — Socio-economic Realities. *ISBN 81-7141-524-3.*

*Vol. 4* HIV/AIDS — Law Ethics and Human Rights, *2 parts. ISBN 81-7141-526-1.*

*Vol. 5* AIDS and NGOs. *ISBN 81-7141-527-X.*

*Vol. 6* AIDS and Home Care. *ISBN 81-7141-528-8.*

*Vol. 7* STD Case Management. *ISBN 81-7141-529-6.*

*Vol. 8* HIV/AIDS Prevention and Care — Teaching Modules for Nurses and Midwives. *ISBN 81-7141-530-X.*

*Vol. 9* HIV Prevention Education for Educational Institutions. *ISBN 81-7141-531-8.*

*Vol.10* Instructional Modules for AIDS Education. *ISBN 81-7141-532-6.*

*Vol.11* School Health Education to Prevent AIDS and STD — A Package for Curriculum Planners. I*SBN 81-7141-533-4.*

Bhaskara Rao, Digumarti, Editor (2000). *International Encyclopaedia of Human Rights*, 7 Volumes in 13 Parts. New Delhi: Discovery Publishing House. ISBN 81-7141-567-9 (set).

*Vol. 1* International Instruments of Human Rights, *2 Parts. ISBN 81-7141-569-4.*

*Vol. 2* Regional Instruments of Human Rights. *ISBN 81-7141-604-7.*

*Vol. 3* Human Rights and the United Nations, *2 Parts. ISBN 81-7141-605-5.*

*Vol. 4* Fact Files of Human Rights*, 3 Parts. ISBN 81-7141-606-3.*

*Vol. 5* Study Stories of Human Rights*, 3 Parts. ISBN 81-7141-607-3.*

*Vol. 6 I*nternational Meetings on Human Rights, *2 Parts. ISBN 81-714-608-X.*

*Vol. 7* Professional Training in Human Rights. I*SBN 81-7141-609-8.*

Bhaskara Rao, Digumarti, Editor (2000). *International Encyclopaedia of Science and Technology Education,* 11 Volumes. New Delhi: Discovery Publishing House. ISBN 81-7141-548-2 (set).

*Vol. 1* Science and Technology Education. *ISBN 81-7141-568-7.*

*Vol. 2* Science Education in Developing Countries. *ISBN 81-7141-569-9.*

*Vol. 3* Organizational Structure of Science. *ISBN 81 7141-570-9.*

*Vol. 4 S*cience Education in Asia and the Pacific. *ISBN 81-7141-571-7.*

*Vol. 5* Science and Technology Education For All. *ISBN 81-7141-572-5.*

*Vol. 6* Values, Ethics, Talent and Girls in Science and Technology Education. *ISBN 81-7141-573-3.*

*Vol. 7* Popularization of Science and Technology Education. *ISBN 81-7141-574-1.*

*Vol. 8* Science, Power and Society. *ISBN 81-7141-575-X.*

*Vol. 9* Information Technology. *ISBN 81-7141-576-8.*

*Vol. 10* Teacher Training in Science and Technology Education. *ISBN 81-7142-577-6.*

*Vol.11* Teacher Training in Science and Technology: A Curriculum Framework. *ISBN 81-7141-578-4.*

Bhaskara Rao, Digumarti, Editor (2000). *Education For All: Achieving the Goal*, 3 Volumes. New Delhi: APH Publishing Corporation. ISBN 81-7648-152-1 (set).

*Vol. I* The Global Consensus. *ISBN 81-7648-155-6.*

*Vol. II* Mid-decade Review Reports of Regional Seminars. *ISBN 81-7648-154-8.*

*Vol. III Issues and Trends. ISBN 81-7648-155-6.*

Bhaskara Rao, Digumarti, Editor (2004). *International Encyclopaedia of Learning to Live Together*, 4 Volumes. New Delhi: Discovery Publishing House. ISBN 81-7141-848-1.

*Vol. 1* International Conference on Learning to Live Together.

*Vol. 2* Globalization and Living Together.

*Vol. 3* Curriculum for Learning to Live Together.

*Vol. 4* Science Education for the Contemporary Society.

Bhaskara Rao, Digumarti, Editor (2005). *Encyclopaedia of Education for All*, 3 Volumes. New Delhi: Discovery Publishing House. ISBN 81-7141-647-0 (set).

Bhaskara Rao, Digumarti, Editor (2007). *Encyclopaedia of Teacher Education,* 4 Volumes. New Delhi: Discovery Publishing House. ISBN 81-8356-306-6 (set).

Bhaskara Rao, Digumarti, Editor (2007). *Encyclopaedia of Edeucation for Living Together,* 4 Volumes. New Delhi: Discovery Publishing House. ISBN 81-7141-848-1 (set).

Bhaskara Rao, Digumarti, Editor (1996). *National Policy on Education,* 2 Volumes. New Delhi: Anmol Publications Pvt. Ltd. ISBN 81-7488-323-1.

Bhaskara Rao, Digumarti, Editor (1996). *Global Perceptions on Peace Education,* 3 Volumes. New Delhi: Discovery Publishing House. ISBN 81-7141-319-6.

Bhaskara Rao, Digumarti, Editor (1997). *Education for the 21st Century.* New Delhi: Discovery Publishing House. ISBN 81-7141-389-7.

Bhaskara Rao, Digumarti, Editor (1997). *Reflections on Scientific Attitude.* New Delhi: Discovery Publishing House. ISBN 81-7141-319-6.

Bhaskara Rao, Digumarti, Editor (1997). *Success Story of a Primary Education Project.* New Delhi: APH Publishing Corporation. ISBN 81-7024-850-7.

Bhaskara Rao, Digumarti, Editor (1997). *World Food Summit.* New Delhi: Discovery Publishing House. ISBN 81-7141-386-2.

Bhaskara Rao, Digumarti, Editor (1997). *Care the Child,* 2 Volumes. New Delhi: Discovery Publishing House. ISBN 81-7141-394-3.

Bhaskara Rao, Digumarti, Editor (1998). *Earth Summit,* 2 Volumes. New Delhi: Discovery Publishing House. ISBN 81-7141-435-4.

Bhaskara Rao, Digumarti, Editor (1998). *Adolescence Education.* New Delhi: Discovery Publishing House. ISBN 81-7141-432-X.

Bhaskara Rao, Digumarti, Editor (1998). *Community and School Nutrition Education.* New Delhi: Discovery Publishing House. ISBN 81-7141-435-4.

Bhaskara Rao, Digumarti, Editor (1998). *District Primary Education Programme.* New Delhi: Discovery Publishing House. ISBN 81-7141-396-X.

Bhaskara Rao, Digumarti, Editor (1998). *National Policy on Education: Towards an Enlightened and Humane Society.* New Delhi: Discovery Publishing House. ISBN 81-7141-426-5.

Bhaskara Rao, Digumarti, Editor (1998). *Reforming School Education.* New Delhi: Discovery Publishing House. ISBN 81-7141-403-6.

Bhaskara Rao, Digumarti, Editor (1998). *Teacher Education in India.* New Delhi: Discovery Publishing House. ISBN 81-7141-406-0.

Bhaskara Rao, Digumarti, Editor (1998). *World Summit for Social Development.* New Delhi: Discovery Publishing House. ISBN 81-7141-420-6.

Bhaskara Rao, Digumarti, Editor (2001). *Nuclear Materials: Issues and Concerns,* 2 Volumes. New Delhi: Discovery Publishing House. ISBN 81-7141-611-X.

Bhaskara Rao, Digumarti, Editor (2001). *Distance Education in Different Countries.* New Delhi: APH Publishing Corporation. ISBN 81-7648-229-3.

Bhaskara Rao, Digumarti, Editor (2001). *Decentralised Management of Education: Management of Education in Panchayati Raj and Municipal Bodies.* New Delhi: Discovery Publishing House. ISBN 81-7141-617-9.

Bhaskara Rao, Digumarti, Editor (2001). *Electrochemistry for Environmental Protection.* New Delhi: Discovery Publishing House. ISBN 81-7141-619-5.

Bhaskara Rao, Digumarti, Editor (2001). *Global Educational Studies.* New Delhi: Discovery Publishing House. ISBN 81-7141-616-0.

Bhaskara Rao, Digumarti, Editor (2001). *Global Synthesis of Educational Assessment.* New Delhi: Discovery Publishing House. ISBN 81-7141-613-6.

Bhaskara Rao, Digumarti, Editor (2001). *Jomtein Decade of Education.* New Delhi: Discovery Publishing House. ISBN 81-7141-618-7.

Bhaskara Rao, Digumarti, Editor (2001). *World Conference on Higher Education.* New Delhi: Discovery Publishing House. ISBN 81-7141-610-1.

Bhaskara Rao, Digumarti, Editor (2001). *World Conference on Science.* New Delhi: Discovery Publishing House. ISBN 81-7141-612-8.

Bhaskara Rao, Digumarti, Editor (2003). *Inspiring Experiences in Teacher Education.* New Delhi: Discovery Publishing House. ISBN 81-7141-656-X.

Bhaskara Rao, Digumarti, Editor (2003). *International Studies in Education,* 3 Volumes. New Delhi: Discovery Publishing House. ISBN 81-7141-647-0.

Bhaskara Rao, Digumarti, Editor (2003). *Military Conversion: Impact on Science and Technology.* New Delhi: Discovery Publishing House. ISBN 81-7141-578-4.

Bhaskara Rao, Digumarti, Editor (2003). *United Nations Millennium Summit.* New Delhi: Discovery Publishing House. ISBN 81-7141-632-2.

Bhaskara Rao, Digumarti, Editor (2003). *World Assembly on Aging.* New Delhi: Discovery Publishing House. ISBN 81-7141-637-3.

Bhaskara Rao, Digumarti, Editor (2003). *World Conference on Human Rights.* New Delhi: Discovery Publishing House. ISBN 81-7141-661-6.

Bhaskara Rao, Digumarti, Editor (2003). *World Education Forum.* New Delhi: Discovery Publishing House. ISBN 81-7141-639-X.

Bhaskara Rao, Digumarti, Editor (2003). *Education, Employment and Human Resource Development.* New Delhi: Discovery Publishing House. ISBN 81-7141-681-0.

Bhaskara Rao, Digumarti, Editor (2003). *Successful Schooling.* New Delhi: Discovery Publishing House. ISBN 81-7141-677-2.

Bhaskara Rao, Digumarti, Editor (2003). *European Education and Teachers.* New Delhi: Discovery Publishing House. ISBN 81-7141-702-7.

Bhaskara Rao, Digumarti, Editor (2003). *Teachers in a Changing World.* New Delhi: Discovery Publishing House. ISBN 81-7141-694-2.

Bhaskara Rao, Digumarti, Editor (2004). *International Guidelines on Open and Distance Teacher Education.* New Delhi: Discovery Publishing House. ISBN 81-7141-777-9.

Bhaskara Rao, Digumarti, Editor (2004). *Adult Learning in the 21st Century.* New Delhi: Discovery Publishing House. ISBN 81-7141-797-3.

Bhaskara Rao, Digumarti, Editor (2004). *Educational Practices: Research and Recommendations.* New Delhi: Discovery Publishing House. ISBN 81-7141-835-X.

Bhaskara Rao, Digumarti, Editor (2004). *General Secondary Education In the 21st Century.* New Delhi: Discovery Publishing House.

Bhaskara Rao, Digumarti, Editor (2004). *Reforming Secondary Education.* New Delhi: Discovery Publishing House. ISBN 81-7141-843-0.

Bhaskara Rao, Digumarti, Editor (2004). *Human Rights Education.* New Delhi: Discovery Publishing House. ISBN 81-7141-882-1.

Bhaskara Rao, Digumarti, Editor (2004). *United Nations Decade for Human Rights Education.* New Delhi: Discovery Publishing House. ISBN 81-7141-887-2.

Bhaskara Rao, Digumarti, Editor (2004). *Technical and Vocational Education and Training in the 21st Century.* New Delhi: Discovery Publishing House. ISBN 81-7141-984-4.

Bhaskara Rao, Digumarti, Editor (2005). *Encyclopaedia of Education For All,* 3 Volumes. New Delhi: Discovery Publishing House.

Bhaskara Rao, Digumarti, Editor (2011). *Right to Education.* Hyderabad: Neel Kamal Publishers. ISBN 978-81-8316-284-5.

Bhaskara Rao, Digumarti, Editor (2011). *International Encyclopaedia of Educational Policies.* Hyderabad: Neel Kamal Publishers.

Bhaskara Rao, Digumarti, Editor (2011). *International Encyclopaedia of Educational Practices.* Hyderabad: Neel Kamal Publishers.

Bhaskara Rao, Digumarti and B.S.V. Dutt, Editors (2003). *Education: Programmes and Policies.* New Delhi: APH Publishing Corporation. ISBN 81-7648-470-9.

Bhaskara Rao, Digumarti, C.A.P. Swamy and B.S.V. Dutt (1997). *Self-Evaluation in Student Teaching.* New Delhi: Discovery Publishing House. ISBN 81-7141-374-9.

Bhaskara Rao, Digumarti and C. D. Swarna Lattha, Editors (2006). *Encyclopaedia of Biotechnology,* 5 Volumes. New Delhi: Discovery Publishing House. ISBN 81-8356-168-3 (set).

Bhaskara Rao, Digumarti, C. Sridevi and K. Vijaya (1995). *Achievement in Social Studies.* New Delhi: Discovery Publishing House. ISBN 81-7141-281-5.

Bhaskara Rao, Digumarti and D. Naresh Kumar (2004). *School Teacher Effectiveness.* New Delhi: Discovery Publishing House. ISBN 81-7141-785-5.

Bhaskara Rao, Digumarti and D. Sridhar (2002). *Job Satisfaction of School Teachers.* New Delhi: Discovery Publishing House. ISBN 81-7141-652-7.

Bhaskara Rao, Digumarti and Digumarti Pushpa Latha, Editors (1998). *International Encyclopaedia of Women,* 5 Volumes. New Delhi: Discovery Publishing House. ISBN 81-7141-410-9 (set).

*Vol. 1* *Status of World's Women.* ISBN 81-7141-494-X.

*Vol. 2* *Women, Education and Empowerment.* ISBN 81-7141-498-1.

*Vol. 3* *Women Challenges and Advancement.* ISBN 81-7141-497-4.

*Vol. 4* *Women and Family Health.* ISBN 81-7141-497-4.

*Vol. 5* *Women and International Action.* ISBN 81-7141-498-2.

Bhaskara Rao, Digumarti and Digumarti Pushpa Latha (1994). *Achievement in Biology.* New Delhi: Discovery Publishing House. ISBN 81-7141-264-5.

Bhaskara Rao, Digumarti and Digumarti Pushpa Latha (1995). *Achievement in English.* New Delhi: Discovery Publishing House. ISBN 81-7141-283-1.

Bhaskara Rao, Digumarti and Digumarti Pushpa Latha (1994). *Achievement in Science.* New Delhi: Discovery Publishing House. ISBN 81-7141-280-70.

Bhaskara Rao, Digumarti and Digumarti Pushpa Latha (1995). *Achievement in Mathematics.* New Delhi: Discovery Publishing House. ISBN 81-7141-278-5.

Bhaskara Rao, Digumarti and Digumarti Pushpa Latha (2004). *Education for Women.* New Delhi: Discovery Publishing House. ISBN 81-7141-873-2.

Bhaskara Rao, Digumarti, Digumarti Pushpa Latha and Digumarthi Harshitha, Editors (2001). *Biological Warfare.* New Delhi: Discovery Publishing House. ISBN 81-7141-597-0.

Bhaskara Rao, Digumarti, Digumarti Pushpa Latha and Digumarthi Harshitha, Editors (2001). *Women as Educators.* New Delhi: Discovery Publishing House. ISBN 81-7141-602-0.

Bhaskara Rao, Digumarti and Digumarthi Harshitha (2004). *Adjustment of Adolescents.* New Delhi: APH Publishing House. ISBN 81-7648-836-8.

Bhaskara Rao, Digumarti and Digumarthi Harshitha, Editors (2001). *Education in India.* New Delhi: APH Publishing House. ISBN 81-7648-207-2.

Bhaskara Rao, Digumarti, Digumarti Pushpa Latha and Digumarthi Harshitha, Editors (2001). *Assessing Learning Achievement.* New Delhi: Discovery Publishing House. ISBN 81-7141-601-2.

Bhaskara Rao, Digumarti, Digumarti Pushpa Latha and Digumarthi Harshitha, Editors (2001). *Energy Security.* New Delhi: Discovery Publishing House. ISBN 81-7141-598-9.

Bhaskara Rao, Digumarti, Digumarthi Harshitha and K.R.S. Sambasiva Rao, Editors (1999). *Advanced Biotechnology.* New Delhi: Discovery Publishing House. ISBN 81-7141-516-4.

Bhaskara Rao, Digumarti and K.R.S. Sambasiva Rao, Editors (1996). *Current Trends in Indian Education.* New Delhi: Discovery Publishing House. ISBN 81-7141-311-0.

Bhaskara Rao, Digumarti and D. Naresh Kumar (2004). *School Teacher Effectiveness.* New Delhi: Discovery Publishing House. ISBN 81-7141-782-5.

Bhaskara Rao, Digumarti and E. Sreekanth Babu (2004). *Educational Interests of School Students.* New Delhi: Discovery Publishing House. ISBN 81-7141-837-6.

Bhaskara Rao, Digumarti and K. Vijaya (1995). *A Text Book Evaluation.* Ambala Cantt: The Associated Publishers.

Bhaskara Rao, Digumarti and M.A. Fayaz (2004). *Problems of Primary School Drop-outs.* New Delhi: Discovery Publishing House. ISBN 81-7141-834-1.

Bhaskara Rao, Digumarti and N.V.M. Mohana Rao (2002). *Problems of Mentally Handicapped Children.* New Delhi: Discovery Publishing House. ISBN 81-7141-645-4.

Bhaskara Rao, Digumarti and S. Chandra Mohan (2002). *Sports Management.* New Delhi: APH Publishing House. ISBN 81-7648-467-9.

Bhaskara Rao, Digumarti and S.A. Khader (2004). *Problems of Private School Teachers.* New Delhi: Discovery Publishing House. ISBN 81-7141-838-4.

Bhaskara Rao, Digumarti and S.A. Khader (2004). *School Education in India.* New Delhi: Discovery Publishing Corporation. ISBN 81-7141-849-X.

Bhaskara Rao, Digumarti and Sk. Johni Basha (2004). *Teachers' Population Education Awareness.* New Delhi: Discovery Publishing House. ISBN 81-7141-832-5.

Bhaskara Rao, Digumarti, V.V. Rao, V.V. Lakshmi and V.V. Krishna, Editors (1999). *Status and Advancement of Women.* New Delhi: APH Publishing Corporation. ISBN 81-7648-169-6.

Amala, P.A. and Anupama, P., Authors and Digumarti Bhaskara Rao, Editor (2004). *History of Education.* New Delhi: Discovery Publishing House. ISBN 81-7141-860-0.

Babu, P.C., Author and Digumarti Bhaskara Rao, Editor (2004). *Flowers of Wisdom.* New Delhi: Discovery Publishing House. ISBN 81-7141-695-0.

Bujji Babu, K., Author and Digumarti Bhaskara Rao, Editor (2007). *Teaching Aptitude of Primary School Teachers.* New Delhi: Sonali Publications. ISBN 81-8411-083-9.

Appala Naidu, P.Ch., Author and Digumarti Bhaskara Rao, Editor (2007). *Student Feedback Methods.* New Delhi: Discovery Publishing House.

Bhagya Lakshmi, L., Author and Digumarti Bhaskara Rao, Editor (2000). *Reading and Comprehension.* New Delhi: Discovery Publishing House. ISBN 81-7141-543-1.

Bhasha, S.A., Author and Digumarti Bhaskara Rao, Editor (2004). *Methods of Teaching Geography.* New Delhi: Discovery Publishing House. ISBN 81-7141-807-4.

Bhuvaneswara Lakshmi, Gadde, Author and Digumarti Bhaskara Rao, Editor(2000). *Attitude Towards Science.* New Delhi: Discovery Publishing House. ISBN 81-7141-541-6.

Bhuvaneswara Lakshmi, G., Author and Digumarti Bhaskara Rao, Editor (2004). *Methods of Teaching Life Science.* New Delhi: Discovery Publishing House. ISBN 81-7141-804-X.

Bhuvaneswara Lakshmi, G. and K. Subba Rao, Authors and Digumarti Bhaskara Rao, Editor (2004). *Methods of Teaching Biology.* New Delhi: Discovery Publishing House. ISBN 81-7141-914-3.

Chary, K.V.N.B., Author and Digumarti Bhaskara Rao, Editor (2006). *Techniques of Teaching Physics.* New Delhi: Sonali Publications. ISBN 81-8411-046-4.

Chowdary, S.B.J.R. and Naga Raju, Authors and Digumarti Bhaskara Rao, Editor (2004). *Mastery of Teaching Skills.* New Delhi: Discovery Publishing House. ISBN 81-7141-861-9.

Dayakara Reddy, V. and Digumarti Bhaskara Rao, Editors (2006). *Value-oriented Education.* New Delhi: Discovery Publishing House. ISBN 81-8356-051-2.

Devraj, T.A.S., Author and Digumarti Bhaskara Rao, Editor (1997). *Trace Analysis of Uranium and Thorium.* New Delhi: Discovery Publishing House. ISBN 81-7141-375-7.

Durga Rani, K., Author and Digumarti Bhaskara Rao, Editor (2000). *Educational Aspirations and Scientific Attitudes.* New Delhi: Discovery Publishing House. ISBN 81-7141-555-5.

Dutt, B.S.V. and Digumarti Bhaskara Rao (2001). *Empowering Primary Teachers.* New Delhi: Discovery Publishing House. ISBN 81-7141-615-2.

Dutt, B.S.V., Author and Digumarti Bhaskara Rao, Editor (2004). *Comparative Education.* New Delhi: Discovery Publishing House. ISBN 81-7141-912-7.

Ediger, Marlow and Digumarti Bhaskara Rao, Editors (2006). *Encyclopaedia of School Education,* 5 Volumes. New Delhi: Discovery Publishing House. ISBN 81-8356-308-2 (set).

Ediger, Marlow and Digumarti Bhaskara Rao, Editors (2006). *Encyclopaedia of School Administration,* 4 Volumes. New Delhi: Discovery Publishing House. ISBN 81-8356-307-4 (set).

Ediger, Marlow and Digumarti Bhaskara Rao, Editors (2007). *Encyclopaedia of School Curriculum,* 10 Volumes. New Delhi: Discovery Publishing House. ISBN 81-8356-305-8 (set).

Ediger, Marlow and Digumarti Bhaskara Rao, Editors (2007). *Encyclopaedia of Teaching,* 8 Volumes. New Delhi: Discovery Publishing House. ISBN 81-8356-305-8 (set).

Marlow Ediger and Digumarti Bhaskara Rao, Editors (2006). *Encyclopaedia of School Education,* 5 Volumes. New Delhi: Discovery Publishing House. ISBN 81-8356-308-2 (set).

Marlow Ediger and Digumarti Bhaskara Rao, Editors (2006). *Encyclopaedia of School Administration,* 4 Volumes. New Delhi: Discovery Publishing House. ISBN 81-8356-307-4 (set).

Marlow Ediger and Digumarti Bhaskara Rao, Editors (2007). *Encyclopaedia of School Curriculum,* 10 Volumes. New Delhi: Discovery Publishing House. ISBN 81-8356-305-8 (set).

Marlow Ediger and Digumarti Bhaskara Rao, Editors (2007). *Encyclopaedia of Teaching,* 8 Volumes. New Delhi: Discovery Publishing House. ISBN 81-8356-305-8 (set).

Ediger, Marlow and Digumarti Bhaskara Rao (1996). *Science Curriculum.* New Delhi: Discovery Publishing House. ISBN 81-7141-321-8.

Ediger, Marlow and Digumarti Bhaskara Rao (2000). *Teaching Mathematics Successfully.* New Delhi: Discovery Publishing House. ISBN 81-7141-552-0.

Ediger, Marlow and Digumarti Bhaskara Rao (2001). *Teaching Science Successfully.* New Delhi: Discovery Publishing House. ISBN 81-7141-600-4.

Ediger, Marlow and Digumarti Bhaskara Rao (2001). *Teaching Social Studies Successfully.* New Delhi: Discovery Publishing House. ISBN 81-7141-596-2.

Ediger, Marlow and Digumarti Bhaskara Rao (2002). *Philosophy and Curriculum.* New Delhi: Discovery Publishing House. ISBN 81-7141-631-4.

Ediger, Marlow and Digumarti Bhaskara Rao (2002). *Improving School Administration.* New Delhi: Discovery Publishing House. ISBN 81-7141-633-0.

Ediger, Marlow and Digumarti Bhaskara Rao (2002). *Elementary Curriculum.* New Delhi: Discovery Publishing House. ISBN 81-7141-658-6.

Ediger, Marlow and Digumarti Bhaskara Rao (2003). *Language Arts Curriculum.* New Delhi: Discovery Publishing House. ISBN 81-7141-657-8.

Ediger, Marlow and Digumarti Bhaskara Rao (2003). *Psychology and Curriculum.* New Delhi: Discovery Publishing House. ISBN 81-7141-691-8.

Ediger, Marlow and Digumarti Bhaskara Rao (2003). *Teaching Language Arts Successfully.* New Delhi: Discovery Publishing House. ISBN 81-7141-678-0.

Ediger, Marlow and Digumarti Bhaskara Rao (2003). *School Curriculum and Administration.* New Delhi: Discovery Publishing House. ISBN 81-7141-709-4.

Ediger, Marlow and Digumarti Bhaskara Rao (2003). *Teaching Mathematics in Elementary Schools.* New Delhi: Discovery Publishing House. ISBN 81-7141-687-X.

Ediger, Marlow and Digumarti Bhaskara Rao (2003). *Teaching Science in Elementary Schools.* New Delhi: Discovery Publishing House. ISBN 81-7141-698-5.

Ediger, Marlow and Digumarti Bhaskara Rao (2003). *School Curriculum and Administration.* New Delhi: Discovery Publishing House. ISBN 81-7141-709-4.

Ediger, Marlow and Digumarti Bhaskara Rao (2003). *Elementary Curriculum Improvement.* New Delhi: Discovery Publishing House. ISBN 81-7141-740-X.

Ediger, Marlow and Digumarti Bhaskara Rao (2004). *School Organisation.* New Delhi: Discovery Publishing House. ISBN 81-7141-843-0.

Ediger, Marlow and Digumarti Bhaskara Rao (2004). *Relevancy in Elementary Curriculum.* New Delhi: Discovery Publishing House. ISBN 81-7141-845-9.

Ediger, Marlow and Digumarti Bhaskara Rao (2005). *Quality School Education.* New Delhi: Discovery Publishing House. ISBN 81-8356-022-9.

Ediger, Marlow and Digumarti Bhaskara Rao (2006). *Successful School Education*. New Delhi: Discovery Publishing House. ISBN 81-8356-054-7.

Ediger, Marlow and Digumarti Bhaskara Rao (2006). *Successful School Administration*. New Delhi: Discovery Publishing House. ISBN 81-8356-046-6.

Ediger, Marlow and Digumarti Bhaskara Rao (2006). *Issues in School Curruculum*. New Delhi: Discovery Publishing House. ISBN 81-8356-052-0.

Ediger, Marlow and Digumarti Bhaskara Rao (2006). *Community College — Curriculum and Teaching*. New Delhi: Discovery Publishing House. ISBN 81-8356-053-9.

Ediger, Marlow and Digumarti Bhaskara Rao (2006). *Administration of Schools*. New Delhi: Discovery Publishing House.

Ediger, Marlow and Digumarti Bhaskara Rao (2006). *Reading Curriculum and Instruction*. New Delhi: Discovery Publishing House.

Ediger, Marlow and Digumarti Bhaskara Rao (2006). *Curriculum Organisation*. New Delhi: Discovery Publishing House.

Ediger, Marlow and Digumarti Bhaskara Rao (2006). *Curriculum of School Subjects*. New Delhi: Discovery Publishing House.

Ediger, Marlow, B.S.V. Dutt and Digumarti Bhaskara Rao (2003). *Teaching English Successfully*. New Delhi: Discovery Publishing House. ISBN 81-7141-707-8.

Ediger, Marlow and Digumarti Bhaskara Rao (2007). *School Science Education*. New Delhi: Discovery Publishing House. ISBN 81-8356-352-X.

Ediger, Marlow and Digumarti Bhaskara Rao (2007). *Language Arts Education*. New Delhi: Discovery Publishing House. ISBN 81-8356-333-3.

Ediger, Marlow and Digumarti Bhaskara Rao (2010). *Effective Schooling.* New Delhi: Discovery Publishing House. ISBN 978-81-8356-613-1.

Ediger, Marlow and Digumarti Bhaskara Rao (2010). *Effective School Curriculum.* New Delhi: Discovery Publishing House. ISBN 978-81-8356-585-1.

Ediger, Marlow and Digumarti Bhaskara Rao (2010). *Essays on Teaching Science.* New Delhi: Discovery Publishing House Pvt. Ltd. ISBN 978-81-8356-882-1.

Ediger, Marlow and Digumarti Bhaskara Rao (2010). *Essays on Teaching Social Studies.* New Delhi: Discovery Publishing House Pvt. Ltd. ISBN 978-81-8356-883-8.

Ediger, Marlow and Digumarti Bhaskara Rao (2010). *Essays on Teaching Reading.* New Delhi: Discovery Publishing House Pvt. Ltd. ISBN 978-81-8356-881-4.

Ediger, Marlow and Digumarti Bhaskara Rao (2010). *Essays on Teaching Mathematics.* New Delhi: Discovery Publishing House Pvt. Ltd. ISBN 978-81-8356-880-7.

Elizabeth, M.E.S., Author and Digumarti Bhaskara Rao, Editor (2004). *Methods of Teaching English.* New Delhi: Discovery Publishing House. ISBN 81-7141-809-0.

Elizabeth, M.E.S., Author and Digumarti Bhaskara Rao, Editor (2004). *Acquisition of English Vocabulary.* New Delhi: Discovery Publishing House. ISBN 81-8356-075-X

Fatima, Sk. Author and Digumarti Bhaskara Rao, Editor (2007). *Reasoning Ability of School Students.* New Delhi: Discovery Publishing House. ISBN 81-8356-330-9.

Gopala Krishna, M., Author and Digumarti Bhaskara Rao, Editor (2007). *Techniques of Teaching Physical Education.* New Delhi: Sonali Publications. ISBN 81-8411-044-8.

Gopala Krishna, M., Author and Digumarti Bhaskara Rao, Editor (2007). *Techniques of Teaching Education.* New Delhi: Sonali Publications. ISBN 81-8411-062-6.

Harshitha, Digumarthi, Author and Digumarti Bhaskara Rao, Editor (2004). *Methods of Teaching Information Technology.* New Delhi: Discovery Publishing House. ISBN 81-7141-805-8.

Harshitha, Digumarthi, Author and Digumarti Bhaskara Rao, Editor (2007). *Techniques of Teaching Computer Science.* New Delhi: Sonali Publications. ISBN 81-8411-036-7.

Indira Devi, Author and J. Prasanth Kumar and Digumarti Bhaskara Rao, Editors (2004). *Values in Language Text Books.* New Delhi: Discovery Publishing House. ISBN 81-7141-833-3.

Jalaja Kumari, C., Author and Digumarti Bhaskara Rao, Editor (2004). *Methods of Teaching Educational Technology.* New Delhi: Discovery Publishing House. ISBN 81-7141-810-4.

Jalaja Kumari, C., Author and Digumarti Bhaskara Rao, Editor (2007). *Job Satisfaction of Teachers.* New Delhi: Discovery Publishing House. ISBN 81-8356-329-5.

Janardhan Reddy, B., Author and Digumarti Bhaskara Rao, Editor (2006). *Techniques of Teaching Sociology.* New Delhi: Sonali Publications. ISBN 81-8411-042-1.

Jayasree, K., Author and Digumarti Bhaskara Rao, Editor (1999). *Correlates of Socialisation.* New Delhi: Discovery Publishing House. ISBN 81-7141-517-2.

Jayasree, K., Author and Digumarti Bhaskara Rao, Editor (2004). *Methods of Teaching Science.* New Delhi: Discovery Publishing House. ISBN 81-7141-801-5.

John Babu, C., Author and T.J.R. Prasad, G.M. Madhukar and Digumarti Bhaskara Rao, Editors (2004). *Problem Solving in Mathematics.* New Delhi: APH Publishing Corporation. ISBN 81-7648-273-0.

Joseph Raju, B and G.A. Anitha, Authors and Digumarti Bhaskara Rao, Editor (2004). *Population Education.* New Delhi: Sonali Publications. ISBN 81-88836-31-3.

Jyosthana, M., Author and Digumarti Bhaskara Rao, Editor (2011). *Achievement Motivation and Achievement in English of School Students.* New Delhi: Discovery Publishing House.

Lalitha, T., Author and K.S. Prabhakaram, D.S.N. Sastry and Digumarti Bhaskara Rao, Editors (2004). *Educational Philosophic Beliefs.* New Delhi: Discovery Publishing House. ISBN 81-7141-765-5.

Krishna, G., Author and Digumarti Bhaskara Rao, Editor (2006). *Techniques of Teaching Physical Education.* New Delhi: Sonali Publications. ISBN 81-8411-044-8.

Kumar Raja, G., Author and Digumarti Bhaskara Rao, Editor (2007). *Principles of Primary School.* New Delhi: Sonali Publications. ISBN 81-8411-054-5.

Lakshmi Kumari, V., Author and Digumarti Bhaskara Rao, Editor (2006). *Techniques of Teaching Home Science.* New Delhi: Sonali Publications. ISBN 81-8411-048-0.

Madhava, K., Author and Digumarti Bhaskara Rao, Editor (2008). *Personality of Adolescent Students.* New Delhi: Sonali Publications.

Madhu Bala, Jampala, Author and Digumarti Bhaskara Rao, Editor (2004). *Methods of Teaching Exceptional Children.* New Delhi: Discovery Publishing House. ISBN 81-7141-802-3.

Mallikarjuna Reddy, V., Author and Digumarti Bhaskara Rao, Editor (2011). *Teaching Aptitude, Social Adjustment and Job Satisfaction of Science Teachers.* New Delhi: Discovery Publishing House.

Marja, Talvi and Digumarti Bhaskara Rao, Editors (1996). *Educational Leadership and Social Changes.* New Delhi: Discovery Publishing House. ISBN 81-7141-320-X.

Naga Kumari, U., Author and Digumarti Bhaskara Rao, Editor (2008). *Science Process Skills of School Students*. New Delhi: Discovery Publishing House. ISBN 978-81-8356-263-8.

Nageswara Rao, S. and M. Srihari, Authors and Digumarti Bhaskara Rao, Editor (2004). *Guidance and Counselling*. New Delhi: Discovery Publishing House. ISBN 81-7141-840-6.

Nageswara Rao, S., Author and Digumarti Bhaskara Rao, Editor (2006). *Techniques of Teaching Psychology*. New Delhi: Sonali Publications. ISBN 81-8411-040-5.

Nageswara Rao, S. and P. Sridhar, Authors and Digumarti Bhaskara Rao, Editor (2004). *Methods and Techniques of Teaching*. New Delhi: Sonali Publications. ISBN 81-88836-33-8.

Nirmala Jyothi, M., Author and Digumarti Bhaskara Rao, Editor (2003). *Non-detention System in School Education*. New Delhi: Discovery Publishing House. ISBN 81-7141-654-3.

Padma Tulasi, G., Author and Digumarti Bhaskara Rao, Editor (2004). *Methods of Teaching Elementary Science*. New Delhi: Discovery Publishing House. ISBN 81-7141-871-6.

Pala Prasada Rao, V., Author and K.N. Rani and D. Bhaskara Rao, Editors (2004). *India Pakistan: Partition Perspectives in Indo-English Novels*. New Delhi: Discovery Publishing House. ISBN 81-7141-871-6.

Pala Prasada Rao, V., Author and D. Bhaskara Rao, Editors (2008). *Functioning of Autonomous Colleges*. New Delhi: Discovery Publishing House. ISBN 978-81-8356-258-4.

Pitchi Reddy, M., Author and Digumarti Bhaskara Rao, Editor (2007). *Techniques of Teaching Social Sciences*. New Delhi: Sonali Publications. ISBN 81-8411-066-X.

Prasad Babu, B., Author and P. Madhu and Digumarti Bhaskara Rao, Editors (2006). *Psychological Adjustment and Well-being.* New Delhi: Discovery Publishing House. ISBN 81-8356-204-3.

Prasad Babu, B., Author and M.V.R. Raju and Digumarti Bhaskara Rao, Editors (2006). *Behavioural Problems of School Children.* New Delhi: Discovery Publishing House. ISBN 81-8356-206-X.

Prabhakaram, K.S., Author and Digumarti Bhaskara Rao, Editors (1998). *Concept Attainment Model in Mathematics Teaching.* New Delhi: Discovery Publishing House. ISBN 81-7141-424-9.

Prasanth Kumar, J., Author and Digumarti Bhaskara Rao, Editor (1998). *Effectiveness of Distance Education System.* New Delhi: Discovery Publishing House. ISBN 81-7141-437-0.

Prasanth Kumar, J., Author and Digumarti Bhaskara Rao, Editor (2004). *Methods of Teaching Civics.* New Delhi: Discovery Publishing House. ISBN 81-7141-806-6.

Prasanth Kumar, J., Author and G. Sundara Rao and Digumarti Bhaskara Rao, Editors (2000). *Open University Student Support Services.* New Delhi: Discovery Publishing House. ISBN 81-7141-550-4.

Raja Kumari, M.A. and D.R.S. Sundari, Authors and Digumarti Bhaskara Rao, Editor (2004). *Special Education.* New Delhi: Discovery Publishing House. ISBN 81-7141-846-5.

Raja Kumari, M.A. and D.R.S. Sundari, Authors and Digumarti Bhaskara Rao, Editor (2004). *Methods of Teaching Educational Psychology.* New Delhi: Discovery Publishing House. ISBN 81-7141-820-1.

Ramatulasamma, K., Author and Digumarti Bhaskara Rao, Editor (2002). *Job Satisfaction of Teacher Educators.* New Delhi: Discovery Publishing House. ISBN 81-7141-655-1.

Rama Krishnaiah, D., Author and Digumarti Bhaskara Rao, Editor (1998). *Job Satisfaction of College Teachers.* New Delhi: Discovery Publishing House. ISBN 81-7141-438-9.

Rama Kumar Ratnam, M.V., Author and Digumarti Bhaskara Rao, Editor (1998). *Dukkha: Suffering in Early Buddhism.* New Delhi: Discovery Publishing House. ISBN 81-7141-653-5.

Rama Krishna Prasad and P. Vide Sagar, Authors and Digumarti Bhaskara Rao, Editor (2004). *Methods of Teaching Physical Education.* New Delhi: Discovery Publishing House. ISBN 81-7141-868-6.

Rama Seshaiah, P. Author and Digumarti Bhaskara Rao, Editor (2004). *Methods of Teaching Home Science.* New Delhi: Discovery Publishing House. ISBN 81-7141-916-X.

Rama Swamy, K., Author and Digumarti Bhaskara Rao, Editor (2007). *Techniques of Teaching Environmental Science.* New Delhi: Sonali Publications. ISBN 81-8411-035-9.

Ramesh, A.R., Author and Digumarti Bhaskara Rao, Editor (2006). *Techniques of Teaching Commerce.* New Delhi: Sonali Publications. ISBN 81-8411-043-X.

Ramesh, Ghanta and Digumarti Bhaskara Rao, Editors (1998). *Environmental Education: Problems and Prospects.* New Delhi: Discovery Publishing House. ISBN 81-7141-423-0.

Ranga Rao, B., Author and Digumarti Bhaskara Rao, Editor (2007). *Techniques of Teaching Economics.* New Delhi: Sonali Publications. ISBN 81-8411-056-1.

Ranga Rao, R., Author and Digumarti Bhaskara Rao, Editor (2004). *Methods of Teacher Teaching.* New Delhi: Discovery Publishing House. ISBN 81-7141-812-0.

Rani, S.S., Author and Digumarti Bhaskara Rao, Editor (2006). *Techniques of Teaching Botany.* New Delhi: Sonali Publications. ISBN 81-8411-037-5.

Rathaiah, Lavu and Digumarti Bhaskara Rao, Editors (1996), *International Innovations in Education*. New Delhi: Discovery Publishing House. ISBN 81-7141-359-5.

Rathaiah, Lavu and Digumarti Bhaskara Rao (1997). *Achievement Correlates*. New Delhi: Discovery Publishing House. ISBN 81-7141-385-4.

Ravi Krishna, M., Author and Digumarti Bhaskara Rao, Editor (2004). *Examination System*. New Delhi: Discovery Publishing House. ISBN 81-7141-824-4.

Ravi Kumar, M., Author and Digumarti Bhaskara Rao, Editor (2004). *Methods of Teaching Computer Science*. New Delhi: Discovery Publishing House. ISBN 81-7141-823-6.

Rudramamba, B., Author and Digumarti Bhaskara Rao, Editor (2003). *Problems of Teaching*. New Delhi: APH Publishing Corporation. ISBN 81-7648-462-8.

Rudramamba, B. and V. Lakshmi Kumari, Authors and Digumarti Bhaskara Rao, Editor (2004). *Methods of Teaching Economics*. New Delhi: Discovery Publishing House. ISBN 81-7141-900-3.

Sambasiva Rao, P., Author and Digumarti Bhaskara Rao, Editor (2007). *Techniques of Teaching Psychology*. New Delhi: Sonali Publications. ISBN 81-8411-040-5.

Sanjeeva Rao, P.C., Author and Digumarti Bhaskara Rao, Editor (1996). *A Text Book of Geology*. New Delhi: Discovery Publishing House. ISBN 81-7141-313-7.

Santhanam, T., B. Prasad Babu and S. Sugandhi, Authors and Digumarti Bhaskara Rao, Editor (2007). *Children with Learning Disabilities*. New Delhi: Sonali Publications. ISBN 81-8411-077-4.

Santhanam, T., B. Prasad Babu and S. Sugandhi, Authors and Digumarti Bhaskara Rao, Editor (2008). *Learning Disabilities and Remedial Programmes*. New Delhi: Discovery Publishing House. ISBN 978-81-8356-257-7.

Sarala, M.M.O., Author and Digumarti Bhaskara Rao, Editor (2006). *Techniques of Teaching English.* New Delhi: Sonali Publications. ISBN 81-8411-047-2.

Satya Narayana, G., Author and Digumarti Bhaskara Rao, Editor (2008). *Attitude towards Social Studies and Achievement in Social Studies.* New Delhi: Sonali Publications.

Satya Narayana, V., Author and Digumarti Bhaskara Rao, Editor (2001). *Physical Education, Social Attitudes and Leadership Qualities.* New Delhi: Discovery Publishing House. ISBN 81-7141-593-8.

Satya Narayana, P.V.V. and G. Krishna, Authors and Digumarti Bhaskara Rao, Editor (2004). *Curriculum Development and Management.* New Delhi: Discovery Publishing House. ISBN 81-7141-813-9.

Shamsuddin, Sk. and V. Dayakara Reddy, Authors and Digumarti Bhaskara Rao, Editor (2007). *Values and Academic Achievements.* New Delhi: Discovery Publishing House. ISBN 81-8356-283-3.

Singh, Y.C., Author and Digumarti Bhaskara Rao, Editor (2006). *Techniques of Teaching Science.* New Delhi: Sonali Publications. ISBN 81-8411-041-3.

Sirisha Rani, S., Author and Digumarti Bhaskara Rao, Editor (2007). *Techniques of Teaching Botany.* New Delhi: Sonali Publications. ISBN 81-8411-037-5.

Sivaratnam Reddy, M., Author and Digumarti Bhaskara Rao, Editor (2004). *Creativity in College Students.* New Delhi: Discovery Publishing House. ISBN 81-7141-697-7.

Siva Lakshmi, G.V. and G.L. Subbaiah, Authors and Digumarti Bhaskara Rao, Editor (2004). *Methods of Teaching Environmental Science.* New Delhi: Discovery Publishing House. ISBN 81-7141-839-2.

Srinivas, G. and Digumarti Bhaskara Rao (2007). *Anxiety of Prospective Teachers*. New Delhi: Sonali Publications. ISBN 81-8411-084-7.

Srinivas, G. and Digumarti Bhaskara Rao (2011). *Intelligence and Personality of Prospective Teachers*. New Delhi: Discovery Publishing House.

Srinivas, M. and I. Prasada Rao, Authors and Digumarti Bhaskara Rao, Editor (2004). *Methods of Teaching History*. New Delhi: Discovery Publishing House. ISBN 81-7141-803-1.

Srinivas Rao, P., Author and Digumarti Bhaskara Rao, Editor (2007). *Principles of Secondary School*. New Delhi: Sonali Publications. ISBN 81-8411-058-8.

Srinivasulu, K., Author and Digumarti Bhaskara Rao, Editor (2011). *Achievement Motivation and Academic Achievement of Alcoholic and Non-alcoholic College Students*. New Delhi: Discovery Publishing House Pvt. Ltd. ISBN 978-93-5056-063-1.

Srinivasulu Reddy, M. and K.R.S. Sambasiva Rao, Authors and Digumarti Bhaskara Rao, Editor (1999). *A Text Book of Aquaculture*. New Delhi: Discovery Publishing House. ISBN 81-7141-482-6.

Srinivasa Rao, Mandalapu, Author and Digumarti Bhaskara Rao, Editor (2003). *Achievement Motivation and Achievement in Mathematics*. New Delhi: Discovery Publishing House. ISBN 81-7141-674-8.

Srihari, M., Author and Digumarti Bhaskara Rao, Editor (2003). *Values of Prospective Teachers*. New Delhi: Discovery Publishing House. ISBN 81-8356-328-7.

Subba Rao, K., Author and Digumarti Bhaskara Rao, Editor (2007). *School Education Policy*. New Delhi: Discovery Publishing House. ISBN 81-8356-285-X.

Subba Rao, K., Author and Digumarti Bhaskara Rao, Editor (2007). *Education Planning*. New Delhi: Sonali Publications. ISBN 81-8411-053-7.

Subramanyam, N.R., Author and Digumarti Bhaskara Rao, Editor (2011). *Effectiveness of in-service Training Programmes.* New Delhi: Discovery Publishing House.

Sudhakar Reddy, Y., Author and Digumarti Bhaskara Rao, Editor (2003). *Creativity in Adolescents.* New Delhi: Discovery Publishing House. ISBN 81-7141-659-4.

Sunil Kumar, K. and K. Rama Krishana, Authors and Digumarti Bhaskara Rao, Editor (2004). *Methods of Teaching Chemistry.* New Delhi: Discovery Publishing House. ISBN 81-7141-913-5.

Suneetha, G., Author and Digumarti Bhaskara Rao, Editor (2004). *Environmental Awareness of School Students.* New Delhi: Sonali Publications. ISBN 81-8411-085-5.

Sunita, E. and R. Sambasiva Rao, Authors and Digumarti Bhaskara Rao, Editor (2004). *Methods of Teaching Mathematics.* New Delhi: Discovery Publishing House. ISBN 81-7141-915-1.

Surya Madhava, I., Author and Digumarti Bhaskara Rao, Editor (2006). *Techniques of Teaching Geography.* New Delhi: Sonali Publications. ISBN 81-8411-034-0.

Surya Madhava, I., Author and Digumarti Bhaskara Rao, Editor (2007). *Techniques of Teaching Political Science.* New Delhi: Sonali Publications. ISBN 81-8411-061-8.

Swamy, K.R., Author and Digumarti Bhaskara Rao, Editor (2006). *Techniques of Teaching Environmental Science.* New Delhi: Sonali Publications. ISBN 81-8411-035-9.

Swarna Jyothi, K., Author and Digumarti Bhaskara Rao, Editor (2007). *Educational Research.* New Delhi: Sonali Publications. ISBN 81-8411-063-4.

Swarna Latha, C.D., and Digumarti Bhaskara Rao, Editors (2006). *Encyclopaedia of Biotechnology*, 5 Volumes. New Delhi: Discovery Publishing House. ISBN 81-8356-168-3.

Swarupa Rani, T. and J.R. Priyadarshini, Authors and Digumarti Bhaskara Rao, Editor (2004). *Educational Measurement and Evaluation.* New Delhi: Discovery Publishing House. ISBN 81-7141-859-7.

Vanaja, M., Author and Digumarti Bhaskara Rao, Editor (1999). *Inquiry Training Model.* New Delhi: Discovery Publishing House. ISBN 81-7141-515-6.

Vanaja, M., Author and Digumarti Bhaskara Rao, Editor (2004). *Methods of Teaching Physics.* New Delhi: Discovery Publishing House. ISBN 81-7141-867-8.

Valeri V. Koustiouk, Author and Digumarti Bhaskara Rao, Editor (2002). *A Text Book of Cryogenics.* New Delhi: Discovery Publishing House. ISBN 81-7141-642-X.

Vamsi Krishna, V., Author and Digumarti Bhaskara Rao, Editor (2004). *School Psychology.* New Delhi: Discovery Publishing House. ISBN 81-7141-880-5.

Veena Kumari, Balusu and Digumarti Bhaskara Rao (1996). *Operation Black Board.* New Delhi: Discovery Publishing House. ISBN 81-8356-354-6.

Veena Kumari, Balusu, Author and Digumarti Bhaskara Rao, Editor (2004). *Methods of Teaching Social Studies.* New Delhi: Discovery Publishing House. ISBN 81-7141-899-6.

Veena Kumari, Balusu, Author and Digumarti Bhaskara Rao, Editor (2000). *Psycho-social Correlates of Achievement.* New Delhi: Discovery Publishing House. ISBN 81-7141-547-4.

Venkata Rao, B., Author and Digumarti Bhaskara Rao, Editor (2007). *Techniques of Teaching Chemistry.* New Delhi: Sonali Publications. ISBN 81-8411-057-X.

Venkata Rao, P. and Digumarti Bhaskara Rao (1989). *A Text Book of Zoology — Junior Intermediate.* Guntur: Vignan Publishers.

Venkata Rao, P. and Digumarti Bhaskara Rao (1989). *A Text Book of Zoology — Senior Intermediate.* Guntur: Vignan Publishers.

Venkateswara Rao, V., Author and Digumarti Bhaskara Rao, Editor (2004). *Problems of Education.* New Delhi: Discovery Publishing House. ISBN 81-7141-841-4.

Venkateswara Rao, V., V. Vijaya Lakshmi and V. Vamsi Krishna, Authors and Digumarti Bhaskara Rao, Editor (2004). *Education For All.* New Delhi: Sonali Publications. ISBN 81-88836-30-3.

Venkateswara Rao, V., V. Vijaya Lakshmi and V. Vamsi Krishna, Authors and Digumarti Bhaskara Rao, Editor (2004). *Education in India.* New Delhi: Sonali Publications. ISBN 81-88836-858-9.

Venkateswara Reddy, L. and Narayana, M. L., Authors and Digumarti Bhaskara Rao, Editor (2004). *Education for Dalits.* New Delhi: Discovery Publishing House. ISBN 81-7141-872-4.

Venkateswara Reddy, L. and Narayana, M. L, Authors and Digumarti Bhaskara Rao, Editor (2004). *Methods of Teaching Rural Sociology.* New Delhi: Discovery Publishing House. ISBN 81-7141-811-2.

Venkateswarlu, K. and S.J. Basha, Authors and Digumarti Bhaskara Rao, Editor (2004). *Methods of Teaching Commerce.* New Delhi: Discovery Publishing House. ISBN 81-7141-808-2.

Venugopala Rao, K., Author and Digumarti Bhaskara Rao, Editor (2000). *Teacher Morale in Secondary Schools.* New Delhi: Discovery Publishing House. ISBN 81-7141-551-2.

Venugopala Rao, K., Author and Digumarti Bhaskara Rao, Editor (2007). *Techniques of Teaching History.* New Delhi: Sonali Publications. ISBN 81-8411-059-6.

Vidya, C., Author and Digumarti Bhaskara Rao, Editor (1996). *A Text Book of Nutrition.* New Delhi: Discovery Publishing House. ISBN 81-7141-309-9.

Vimala, T.D., B. Prasad Babu and Digumarti Bhaskara Rao, Editors (2007). *Stress, Coping and Management.* New Delhi: Sonali Publications. ISBN 81-8411-086-3.

Vijaya Bharathi, D., Author and Digumarti Bhaskara Rao, Editor (2000). *Educational Philosophies of Swami Vivekananda and John Dewey.* New Delhi: APH Publishing House. ISBN 81-7648-309-9.

Vijaya Bharathi, D., Author and Digumarti Bhaskara Rao, Editor (2005). *Educational Philosophy of John Dewey.* New Delhi: Discovery Publishing House. ISBN 81-8356-024-5.

Vijaya Bharathi, D., Author and Digumarti Bhaskara Rao, Editor (2005). *Educational Philosophy of Swami Vivekananda.* New Delhi: Discovery Publishing House. ISBN 81-8356-023-7.

Vijaya Lakshmi, D., Author and Digumarti Bhaskara Rao, Editor (2004) *Basic Education.* New Delhi: Discovery Publishing House. ISBN 81-7141-881-3.

Vijaya Lakshmi, V., Author and Digumarti Bhaskara Rao, Editor (2006). *Techniques of Teaching Music.* New Delhi: Sonali Publications. ISBN 81-8411-038-3.

Vijaya Kumar, S.J., Author and Digumarti Bhaskara Rao, Editor (2006). *Techniques of Teaching Mathematics.* New Delhi: Sonali Publications. ISBN 81-8411-039-1.

Visalakshi, V., Author and Digumarti Bhaskara Rao, Editor (2006). *Techniques of Teaching Biology.* New Delhi: Sonali Publications. ISBN 81-8411-045-6.

Visalakshi, V., Author and Digumarti Bhaskara Rao, Editor (2007). *Techniques of Teaching Zoology.* New Delhi: Sonali Publications. ISBN 81-8411-055-3.

**Books in Telugu Language**

Bhaskara Rao, Digumarti (1986). *Dhrushya Sravana Bodhanapakaranalu* (Audio Visual Teaching Aids). Guntur: Nagarjuna Publishers.

Bhaskara Rao, Digumarti (1993). *Jeevasashtra Bodhana* (Teaching of Biology). Guntur: Nagarjuna Publishers.

Bhaskara Rao, Digumarti (1995). *Vignanasasthra Bodhana* (Teaching of science) Guntur: Nagarjuna Publishers.

Bhaskara Rao, Digumarti (1994). *Vidya Manovignana Sastram* (Educational Psychology). Guntur: Nagarjuna Publishers.

Bhaskara Rao, Digumarti (1997). *Vidya Manovignana Sastram* (Educational Psychology). Guntur: Creative Press.

Bhaskara Rao, Digumarti (1998). *DSC Study Material.* Guntur: Nagarjuna Publishers.

Bhaskara Rao, Digumarti (1998). *Upadhyayudu Vidya.* (Teacher and Education) Guntur: Nagarjuna Publishers.

Bhaskara Rao, Digumarti (1998). *Vidya Drukpadalu* (Perspectives of Education). Guntur: Nagarjuna Publishers.

Bhaskara Rao, Digumarti (1999). *EdCET Teaching Aptitude.* Guntur: Nagarjuna Publishers.

Bhaskara Rao, Digumarti (2001). *Bharata Samajamulo Upadyayudu Vidhya* (Teacher and Education in Emerging Indian Society). Guntur: Sri Nagarjuna Publishers.

Bhaskara Rao, Digumarti (2001). *Bhoutika Sastra Bodhana Padhatulu* (Methods of Teaching Physical Science). Guntur: Sri Nagarjuna Publishers.

Bhaskara Rao, Digumarti (2001). *Jeeva Sastra Bodhana Padhatulu* (Methods of Teaching Biology). Guntur: Sri Nagarjuna Publishers.

Bhaskara Rao, Digumarti (2001). *Vidya Manovignana Sastram* (Educational Psychology). Guntur: Sri Nagarjuna Publishers.

Bhaskara Rao, Digumarti (2003). *Patasala Yajamanyam/ Paripalana* (School Management and Administration). Guntur: Sri Nagarjuna Publishers.

Bhaskara Rao, Digumarti and M. Srihari (2009). *Vardamana Bharata Desamulo Vidya* (Education in Emerging India). Guntur: Sri Nagarjuna Publishers.

Bhaskara Rao, Digumarti and B. Prasad Babu (2009). *Vidya Manovignana Sastram* (Educational Psychology). Guntur: Sri Nagarjuna Publishers.

Bhaskara Rao, Digumarti and B. Prasad Babu (2009). *Pradhamika Vidyamariyu Vileena Vidya Dhrukpadhalu* (Perspectives in Primary Education and Inclusive Education). Guntur: Sri Nagarjuna Publishers.

Bhaskara Rao, Digumarti and K. Subba Rao (2009). *Elementary Vidya, Pranalika, Yajamanyam, Upadyaya Kartavyalu* (Elementary Education, Planning, Management and Teacher Functions). Guntur: Sri Nagarjuna Publishers.

Bhaskara Rao, Digumarti and G. Prasanthi (2009). *Samardya Nirmanamu* (Capacity Building). Guntur: Sri Nagarjuna Publishers.

Bhaskara Rao, Digumarti and A. Jagadish (2009). *Vignansastra Bodhana Padhatulu* (Methods of Teaching Science). Guntur: Sri Nagarjuna Publishers.

Bhaskara Rao, Digumarti, Editor (2010). *Vardamana Bharata Desamulo Vidya – D.Ed. Question Bank* (Education in Emerging India). Guntur: Sri Nagarjuna Publishers.

Bhaskara Rao, Digumarti, Editor (2010). *Vidya Manovignana Sastram – D.Ed. Question Bank* (Educational Psychology). Guntur: Sri Nagarjuna Publishers.

Bhaskara Rao, Digumarti, Editor (2010). *Pradhamika Vidya mariyu Vileena Vidya Dhrukpadhalu – D.Ed. Question*

*Bank* (Perspectives in Primary Education and Inclusive Education). Guntur: Sri Nagarjuna Publishers.

Bhaskara Rao, Digumarti, Editor (2010). *Elementary Vidya, Pranalika, Yajamanyam, Upadyaya Kartavyalu – D.Ed. Question Bank* (Elementary Education, Planning, Management and Teacher Functions). Guntur: Sri Nagarjuna Publishers.

Bhaskara Rao, Digumarti, Editor (2010). *Samardya Nirmanamu — D.Ed. Question Bank* (Capacity Building). Guntur: Sri Nagarjuna Publishers.

Bhaskara Rao, Digumarti, Editor (2010). *Ganithasastra Bodhana Padhatulu — D.Ed. Question Bank* (Methods of Teaching Science). Guntur: Sri Nagarjuna Publishers.

Bhaskara Rao, Digumarti, Editor (2010). *Vignansastra Bodhana Padhatulu — D.Ed. Question Bank* (Methods of Teaching Science). Guntur: Sri Nagarjuna Publishers.

Bhaskara Rao, Digumarti, Editor (2010). *Sanghikasastra Bodhana Padhatulu — D.Ed. Question Bank* (Methods of Teaching Social Studies). Guntur: Sri Nagarjuna Publishers.

Bhaskara Rao, Digumarti, Editor (2010). *Telugu Bodhana Padhatulu — D.Ed. Question Bank* (Methods of Teaching Social Studies). Guntur: Sri Nagarjuna Publishers.

Bhaskara Rao, Digumarti, Editor (2010). *Methods of Teaching English — D.Ed. Question Bank*. Guntur: Sri Nagarjuna Publishers.

Bhaskara Rao, Digumarti, Editor (2011). *Vidya Adharalu — B.Ed. Question Bank* (Foundations of Education). Guntur: Sri Nagarjuna Publishers.

Bhaskara Rao, Digumarti, Editor (2011). *Vidya Manovignana Sastram — B.Ed. Question Bank* (Educational Psychology). Guntur: Sri Nagarjuna Publishers.

Bhaskara Rao, Digumarti, Editor (2011). *Vidya Sanketika Sastram and Computer Vidya — B.Ed. Question Bank* (Educational Technology and Computer Education). Guntur: Sri Nagarjuna Publishers.

Bhaskara Rao, Digumarti, Editor (2011). *Patasala Yajamanyam and Systems of Education — B.Ed. Question Bank* (School Management and Computer Education). Guntur: Sri Nagarjuna Publishers.

Bhaskara Rao, Digumarti, Editor (2011). *Personality Development and Communicative English — B.Ed. Question Bank* (Personality Development and Communicative English). Guntur: Sri Nagarjuna Publishers.

Bhaskara Rao, Digumarti, Editor (2011). *Ganithasastra Bodhana Padhatulu — B.Ed. Question Bank* (Methods of Teaching Science). Guntur: Sri Nagarjuna Publishers.

Bhaskara Rao, Digumarti, Editor (2011). *Bhouthika Sastra Bodhana Padhatulu — B.Ed. Question Bank* (Methods of Teaching Science). Guntur: Sri Nagarjuna Publishers.

Bhaskara Rao, Digumarti, Editor (2011). *Jeeva Sastra Bodhana Padhatulu — B.Ed. Question Bank* (Methods of Teaching Science). Guntur: Sri Nagarjuna Publishers.

Bhaskara Rao, Digumarti, Editor (2011). *Sanghikasastra Bodhana Padhatulu — B.Ed. Question Bank* (Methods of Teaching Social Studies). Guntur: Sri Nagarjuna Publishers.

Bhaskara Rao, Digumarti, Editor (2011). *Telugu Bodhana Padhatulu — B.Ed. Question Bank* (Methods of Teaching Social Studies). Guntur: Sri Nagarjuna Publishers.

Bhaskara Rao, Digumarti, Editor (2011). *Methods of Teaching English — B.Ed. Question Bank*. Guntur: Sri Nagarjuna Publishers.

Bhaskara Rao, Digumarti, N. Saraja, J. Lalitha and V. Mrunalini, Translators (2008). *Vidya – Samajam (Education - Society). Hyderabad:* Dr. B. R. Ambedkar Open University.

Gopala Krishna, G., A. Rama Krishna, K. Subba Rao and Bhaskara Rao, Digumarti (2004). *Jeevasashtra Bodhana Padhatulu* (Methods of Teaching of Biological Science). Guntur: Sri Nagarjuna Publishers.

Krishna Murthy, V., K.S. Sudheer Reddy and Digumarti Bhaskara Rao (2004). *Vidya Manovignana Sastra Adharalu* (Foundations of Educational Psychology). Guntur: Sri Nagarjuna Publishers.

Lalini, V., V. Dayakara Reddy, M. Srihari and Digumarti Bhaskara Rao (2004). *Vidya Adharalu* (Foundations of Education). Guntur: Sri Nagarjuna Publishers.

Sastry, G.E.P. and G. Satya Narayana, Authors, Bhaskara Rao, Digumarti, Editor (2009). *Sanghikasastra Bodhana Padhatulu* (Methods of Teaching Social Studies). Guntur: Sri Nagarjuna Publishers.

Subba Rao, K.P., P. Ayodhya and Digumarti Bhaskara Rao (2004). *Patasala Yajamanyam — Vidhya Vyavasthalu* (School Management and Systems of Education). Guntur: Sri Nagarjuna Publishers.

Sudhakar, V., B. Ravindra Babu, D.S. Kumar and Digumarti Bhaskara Rao (2004). *Vidya Sanketika Sastram — Computer Vidhya* (Educational Technology and Computer Education). Guntur: Sri Nagarjuna Publishers.

# Index

## N



## O



## P



## R

**S**



**T**